THE
LEADERSHIP
GENE

THE
LEADERSHIP
GENE

The genetic code
of a life-long
leadership career

Dr CYRIL LEVICKI

FINANCIAL TIMES
PITMAN PUBLISHING

FINANCIAL TIMES

MANAGEMENT

LONDON · SAN FRANCISCO
KUALA LUMPUR · JOHANNESBURG

*Financial Times Management delivers the knowledge,
skills and understanding that enable students,
managers and organisations to achieve their ambitions,
whatever their needs, wherever they are.*

London Office:
128 Long Acre, London WC2E 9AN
Tel: +44 (0)171 447 2000
Fax: +44 (0)171 240 5771
Website: ww.ftmanagement.com

A Division of Financial Times Professional Limited

First published in Great Britain in 1998

ISBN 0 273 63557 3

British Library Cataloguing in Publication Data
A CIP catalogue record for this book can be obtained from
the British Library.

1 3 5 7 9 10 8 6 4 2

Typeset by Northern Phototypesetting Co Ltd, Bolton
Printed and bound in Great Britain by
Biddles Ltd, Guildford and King's Lynn

*The Publishers' policy is to use paper manufactured
from sustainable forests.*

ABOUT THE AUTHOR

Cyril Levicki grew up in London's East End. After leaving school, he worked as a labourer to put money together to start his own business. He also took time out to work with the Save The Children Fund. He spent the next twelve years running his own businesses in retail, wholesale and manufacturing, ranging from a market stall in Petticoat Lane to international import and export.

He became an undergraduate at the age of 32, at London University, gaining a degree in Economics and Politics. Upon leaving, he was awarded a scholarship to research his Ph.D. on leadership decision making at the London Business School. He also taught courses on Advanced Policy and Strategy.

After teaching at the London Business School, he lectured at Cranfield School of Management, before accepting a post as Visiting Professor at Queen Mary College, London University in 1984. He was also appointed Visiting Professor in Strategy at Baruch College (City University of New York) in 1986.

Within a short time he found himself too busy to lecture because of demand in his private consulting practice, which specializes in the development of leaders and their organization strategies at boardroom level. This company also develops senior directors and managers to aid them in the implementation of the strategies which it helps their leaders formulate.

Dr. Levicki has also published *The Theory and Practice of Small Business* and *The Strategy Workout* (1996) which was a semi-finalist in the FT Booz.Allen & Hamilton Global Business Book Awards. It has been reprinted three times in the past twelve months, and has become an international best seller.

Cyril Levicki has acted as consultant to a large variety of international and national corporations, such as APV, BRS, BT, British Gas, Crone Corkhill, Jardine International Insurance, Chloride Batteries, Exel Logistics, Hawker Siddeley, Jones Lang Wootten, Lex Service (Transfleet), L'Oréal, NFC, Protodigm, Reed International, TeleWest Communications, SmithKline Beecham, UCI Logistics and Media One International.

If you would like to contact Cyril Levicki please telephone Omnia Consultants Limited on +44 (0)1869 345210.

This book is dedicated to
my incredibly supportive wife
Phyllis
and my grandson
Oliver

CONTENTS

LIST OF TABLES

LIST OF FIGURES

LIST OF QUESTIONNAIRES

LIST OF CASE STUDIES

ACKNOWLEDGEMENTS

All authors know they owe a debt of thanks to many people. Mine is to the thousands of people whom I have taught in development programmes over the last 17 years, at the London Business School, Cranfield Management School, City University Business School, Queen Mary College, London University, Baruch College, City University of New York and at UMIST. The latter was kind enough to appoint me a Visiting Professorial Fellow in 1997. In addition to my students, I should also acknowledge the hundreds of clients who have employed me as an adviser on strategy, team development and board composition. I feel my debt is the larger because I was learning so much when I was really supposed to be teaching or assisting them! I can only hope that I helped them as much as they taught me of the dynamics and intricacies of leadership. Many of them now lead businesses all over the world. I trust that a few of my values adhered to them.

I also want to thank Richard Stagg and Pradeep Jethi of Financial Times Management. They have been enthusiastic in their support of me in writing this book. They even competed with other publishers, a rare compliment. I must single out Pradeep, however. I have asked other authors and none can match my experience of the intense, profound and immensely helpful editorial feedback he has continuously made to improve the text throughout the writing and production period. If the book is successful, it will owe much to his perspicacious and insightful comments. Thank you, Pradeep.

Finally, I must thank my family. My son, Jeffrey, who at a tender age already understands and allows me to isolate myself in the task of 'getting the book out of my system'. My wife, Phyllis, does much more than proofread my words. She tells me when sentences and paragraphs make no sense; she changes mumbo-jumbo to English; and she allows me the time and space to pursue this strange pastime of trying to write a useful book. I can never thank her enough.

As always, much credit is due to others. As ever, all mistakes are my responsibility. As I state in the book, 'the perfect leader has not yet been born'. I don't think the 'perfect writer' is any more feasible. I hope the reader will forgive my errors because they find enough compensating value to have made reading the book worthwhile.

Dr. Cyril Levicki
May, 1998

INTRODUCTION

There are not many good leaders around. This book is written to try to remedy that situation by helping all those leaders with the leadership gene, to better develop their potential and become one of the leaders who are in such desperately short supply. The title of this book is, of course, not an accident. While there is probably no biological proof that some people are born with a 'leadership gene', I have worked with many senior managers and leaders over the past 20 years, and it has become apparent to me that almost all the leaders I have dealt with have had something very special, a gift, which has singled them out from others. It has been relatively easy to foretell which managers would make the breakthrough to profound leadership skills. This predictability was equally valid for those other managers who could be expected to stay in the 'managerial mode' for the whole of their career.

The sample from which I am making the generalizations in this book was comprised of the thousands of senior managers, and hundreds of leaders, with whom I have worked, either in advanced development programmes, as adviser on strategy; as consultant on top team development; or as personal adviser to the leaders themselves. My clients have included major international and national telecommunications businesses, such as British Telecom, Cable & Wireless, Media One International and One-to-One. In the cable telephony and entertainment industries I have worked with the leaders of international and national majors such as Media One International and TeleWest. In manufacturing and engineering, I have worked with the heads of businesses such as APV, Chloride Batteries, Hawker Siddeley and Reed International. In the world of transport, logistics and distribution I have been adviser and developer to leaders of the NFC (National Freight Consortium), British Road Services, Caliber Logistics, Lynx Express Delivery Services, Ryder International and Exel Logistics. In the world of insurance I have worked with Swiss Re, Guardian Insurance and Jardine International. In the pharmaceutical and ethical products industry, I have worked on strategy and team development with

SmithKline Beecham, Hoffman la Roche (Protodigm, a drugs develop-ment subsidiary), and L'Oréal. I have also advised, at various times, the leaders of businesses such as Jones Lang Wootten (one of the world's largest property consulting businesses) and KPMG Consulting (a world leader in auditing and management consulting). I have conducted inter-national and global strategy and team-assessment assignments through-out the USA, Europe and the Far East. I've been lucky and it's been a lot of fun! It has also given me a unique perspective on the composition and mix of the skills, traits and characteristics of the leaders of many of these organizations.

Let me start by defining the difference between these words, for I shall refer to them constantly throughout the book. Skills are the qualities that any manager can learn, as long as the necessary aptitude is there. These are exemplified in team skills, planning ability or understanding of accounts. Traits are behaviours that result either from training, or habit or inherent received genetic qualities and may be best understood as tendencies or repeated behaviour patterns. Examples of traits are intelligence, equanim-ity, decency and energy. Characteristics are qualities and values which define the actions and styles of high-quality leaders, at all stages of their career. They are the deep-rooted qualities, such as moral fibre, courage, determination to succeed and capacity to inspire, that define great leaders.

I also draw a clear distinction between what I call 'nominal leaders' and 'strategic leaders'. *Nominal leaders* are those people appointed to posts and jobs which call for real leadership but who do not know how to give that leadership. They are, and will always remain, managers. While they can organize others to get things done, they cannot fulfil the ultimate leader-ship role which combines strategic vision, objective judgement and pro-fit-creating business skills. Although 'nominal leaders' are the managerial fabric of every organization, both large and small, they will never become strategic leaders, or movers and shakers. The difficulties arise when, often by accident, sometimes by design, they get into positions which call for real leadership and they prove unable to cope.

In practice, over the years, it has not been difficult to predict fairly cor-rectly the future levels of achievement of most of the managers (therefore, potential leaders) that I have encountered on hundreds of development programmes. The majority of my predictions about who has true leadership skills, have been proven over the 20 years I have been doing this type of work. However, there have been errors of judgement I should like to admit to. One, because I held my incorrect belief about the high quality of the individual for far too long. The other, because my opinion, reported to his human resources director, held back the individual's career for a year or two. However, I would claim that these two examples stand out because they contradict the majority of my predictions. I thought one manager was a leader because he appeared to have moral fibre, decisiveness, insight and strategic vision. He was highly reserved and seemed capable of holding his own counsel so well that I mistook this for the ultimate independence that one sees in all great leaders. Unfortunately, this was a wrong conclusion. His reserve was a result of a real fear that somebody would realize that he had no courage and he was terrified that his colleagues would find out there was almost nothing below the surface. Strangely, in spite of all his colleagues knowing that I admired this man and considered him a winner, they continuously (over a period of 12 years) spoke against this man to me. I considered their criticisms to be inspired by spite and jealousy. I later realized it was because they truly thought I had made an error of judgement. The lesson I learned was that a person's colleagues, even if they themselves are not necessarily equipped with the leadership gene, may still know best who, among themselves, is truly endowed with it.

My other mistake was a happier one. I had been teaching someone on a development programme for managing directors. At the end of the one-year programme I was asked by his human resources director what I thought of him. I replied that he was pleasant and competent but that he was not likely to make it to the upper echelons. Some years later he was appointed managing director. He was successful, not brilliant, but certainly better than I had anticipated. Later he left that company and led a management buyout in another business. Then he really started to flourish. As an entrepreneurial leader he became quite dazzling. It taught me two leasons. The first was that you cannot get it right every time; the second, and more profound lesson, was that there are many different types of leader. Each may be suited to one or two particular types of situation. Until leaders both mature and get themselves into the right business with the needs that they can best fulfil, they may not look like successful leaders at all.

However, these exceptions may be used to prove the rule. In most cases you *can* tell. Elliott Jaques, formerly Director of the Brunel Institute of Social Science and eminent academic authority on predicting leadership and structure, reckoned he could always tell exactly what level a leader would rise to and even when. I do not go that far. I think it is hard to predict the future direction of careers because there are so many accidents that can befall a leader during a career. But, with all other things being equal, I think you can foretell, by and large, that a person has or doesn't have the 'leadership gene'.

There is another underlying theme to this book. It is that leadership and management are in some senses a trade-off, one to another. One might almost say:

'Leaders don't manage and managers don't lead'. (Kotter 1990)

This implies that the roles of leadership and management are almost contradictions of each other. Managers need to be team players. They have to get groups of people to work together to achieve set objectives; they are co-ordinators of others. Leaders, on the other hand, have to satisfy their stakeholders, the people who have power to judge them or have rights over the assets they control. But the leadership job is not just a co-ordination role. Leaders are paid to balance many people's interests as the act of leadership itself. Such leaders must also be visionaries and judges. They have to know how to set examples and to change cultures and atmospheres to evolve the organization into the form it needs to be to achieve their vision of the future. They don't manage people towards a result; they manipulate the entire set of resources – people, assets, streams of income. Leaders have the ultimate responsibility for success. That is the final differentiator between them and managers. Ultimately, all managers have somebody above them who takes responsibility for at least some aspects of their role in the organization. It may be their finance director, their technical research manager or their own line manager who gives them their instructions on strategy. It might be their marketing or sales manager who tells them what to sell and at what price. At the end of the day, there is always somebody else to take the final decision and ultimate responsibility. It is the real leader who, alone, bears total responsibility for the burden of all the facets of the organization's future and its results.

Furthermore, the trade-off between the role of the manager and the role of the leader may well be contra-distinctive of each other. As an individual rises further up the organization, he or she needs to use more leadership skills and fewer management skills, as Figure I.1 illustrates.

Fig. I.1   THE BALANCE BETWEEN MANAGEMENT AND LEADERSHIP OVER TIME

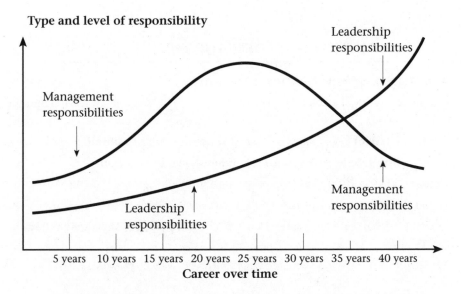

Management responsibilities start early for leaders, in the management phase of their career. It peaks between the 20th and 25th year, for those who are climbing towards a top leadership role. Leadership duties and skills should overtake management tasks, on average, some time in the last 20 per cent of their career.

This book is intended to help you trace the balance which is necessary to retain as you move through the hierarchy towards your personal career goals, either in a senior management role or a leadership role. Somewhere along the road you will realize whether you are 'fit for leadership' as distinct from being 'fit for management'. I sincerely hope that many readers will discover that they have the leadership gene. This book aims to ensure, by the close, that you are better fitted to fulfil your destiny and enjoy your leadership career. Naturally, there will be some among the total readership who won't care to face up to what they discover. They may find they don't really have what it takes to be a strategic leader. But I hope you will.

After all, every leader needs the personal courage it takes to be fully self-aware, even of their own weaknesses. That applies equally to both 'nominal' and 'strategic' leaders. The starting point to build either a management or a leadership career, is one of the absolutes of all great leaders' characteristics, the armour of moral fibre!

For those readers outside the UK, throughout the book I mention the City and City institutions. This refers to London's financial hub, the City of London.

RECOMMENDED READING FOR THE INTRODUCTION

Adair, J. (1988) *Effective Leadership*. London: Pan.

Campbell, A. M., Devine, M., Young, D. (1990) *A Sense of Mission*. London: Hutchinson.

Crainer, S. (1996) *Key Management Ideas*. London: Pitman Publishing.

Ferrucci, P. (1990) *What We May Be*. London: Aquarian/Thorsons.

Herder, J. (1992) *The Tao of Leadership*. Aldershot: Gower.

Jaques, E. (1976) *A General Theory of Bureaucracy*. London: Heinemann.

Kotter, J. (1990) *Force for Change: How Leadership Differs from Management*. Boston: Free Press.

McGregor, D. (1960) *The Human Side of Enterprise*. New York: McGraw-Hill.

WHAT IS A LEADERSHIP CAREER?

....

This chapter will contain definitions of what

we mean by leadership (the role of leading

throughout one's career, ultimately as the main

progenitor in a large economic organization)

It advocates treating leadership as a career

rather than the 'final role'.

....

I'M TALKING TO YOU

Almost everybody who has ever worked in a business organization has pondered whether they could do a better job than the people who lead them. Sometimes it's because they don't understand the complexity of the problems faced by their leaders. At other times it's because the leaders really don't know what they are doing – and don't realize it. Most people have wondered, at some time or other, how good a leader *they* would be if they ran the business. This book is aimed at all those people who are being realistic when they say to themselves, 'when I run this business ...' In my early years as a consultant, I worked mainly with such aspirants and occasionally with their leaders. At that level, it often seemed as if the leaders did not really know what they were doing. As my own career developed I worked increasingly, and then almost exclusively, for those at the top of mainly large corporations, in one-to-one situations, advising on leadership, strategy and top team development. I learned to understand better the pressures and trials of those at the top. I have now spent many years helping leaders of (usually large) businesses to improve their leadership skills, to survive under pressure, and to assess the team around them, when they suspect incompetence. Just occasionally, I have found that it is the leader who has called me in, who is the real problem. More often I find that they need a little help to regain their perspective or equilibrium, following a difficult phase in the life of the business. After nearly 20 years of this kind of work, with some of the largest and most successful businesses in the world, it seems appropriate to describe some of the secrets, necessary skills, traits, characteristics and tricks of 'life at the top'. If you are already there, or hope to be one day, this book is written for you.

> **Most people have wondered, at some time or other, how good a leader *they* would be if they ran the business.**

Let me differentiate immediately between those ultimate leaders of large business organizations who may rightfully be called, 'strategic leaders' and those leaders who have the title but who are what I label 'nominal leaders' – who occupy the space, collect the rewards but who make little ultimate difference to the results of their organizations. All leaders have an enormous responsibility. They accept, sometimes enjoy, great power for substantial rewards. Many people who occupy such positions should never have achieved those heights. Too many people reach the top who should not have succeeded in passing through the eliminating stages of the hierarchy.

A WORKING DEFINITION OF LEADERS AND LEADERSHIP

When one contrasts 'strategic leaders' with what I call 'nominal leaders', people who get to the top but who shouldn't be there, the first thing to say is that the nominal leader knows how to look good. They often have an exaggerated sense of their own skills. They believe they have a right to be 'at the top' and will do whatever it takes to stay there. One often finds that they have enhanced and refined political skills. They needed these skills to get there without any leadership talent. Most people around them can see them for what they are, lacking in leadership skills.

Effective leadership can be displayed at all levels in an organization. I am writing particularly about those who aspire to and actually do lead successfully at the very top of their organization. These are the people that I have been working with, behind the scenes, for the past 15 years. Although it has been my good fortune to have worked with a few, truly great, leaders, I have also, unfortunately, worked with many who can best be described as 'infertile'.

What about this 'leadership gene'?

The oldest intellectual debate in history is whether 'nature' or 'nurture' is the predominant influence on one's behaviour, characteristics, intelligence and achievement levels. There may never be a definitive scientific opinion on this tortuous subject. However, I do offer an opinion on my own special area of leadership. After observing, developing and working alongside many thousands of leaders, I have become convinced that almost all good leaders are born with a special talent, which is modified as they develop as children. The major 'nurture' influencing factors are:

- an unusually dominant mother
- being the eldest child in the family
- having a father who achieved high levels of success (and who manages to make his child like him)
- being chosen by a school teacher for special nurturing.

The problem with a concept such as a 'leadership gene' is that one cannot easily tell if one has it or not. There are signs of it early in a career. What should one look for?

- an independent spirit with good judgement
- special signs of leadership (dignity, easy manners, self-respect, respect for others)
- good relationships with bad managers
- rapid mastery of new tasks and readiness for promotion within a short period after each promotion
- willingness and keenness to learn new things about anything relating to the job
- a contented, well-contained, private life
- attractiveness – everybody wants to be his or her friend.

Try Questionnaire 1.1 to make a first, quick audit of your current suitability or readiness for leadership.

Questionnaire 1.1
AN AUDIT OF LEADERSHIP POTENTIAL

Assess yourself against the listed criteria	High	Score Medium	Low
My speed of mastery of new tasks is			
My feeling that I am always ready to be independent is			
Other's assessment of the objectivity of my judgement is			
People's perception of my level of dignity is			
People would rate the quality of my personal manners as			
I rate my self-respect as			
My respect for others is generally			
My ability to have good relationships with bad managers is			
Up to now, in my career, each promotion has come: high = <2 years; medium = 2–5 years; low = >5 years			
My willingness to learn new things is			
I rate the happiness of my private life as			
My ability to make friends is			
Total: *Score one for each score in each column*			
Apply the multiplier	x 3	x 2	x 1
Final Grand Total			

Interpretation

A score of > 30 points	= high leadership potential
A score between 20 and 29 points	= medium leadership potential
A score of < 20 points	= low leadership potential (but don't stop reading, salvation may lie on the next page)

ARE LEADERS BORN OR ARE THEY MADE?

This question is close to the eternal debate between nature and nurture. But it has enormous importance here. After all, who decides whether you were born to be a leader or not? Once it is decided you are not 'a born leader', what future is there for you, especially if you are only interested in one of the top jobs of business organizations?

I argue that leaders need to be born with a set of genetic characteristics which create the raw materials from which leadership may be nurtured. If the potential is not there, it cannot be developed. I concede that it is not always clear that a person *is* a born leader. This can be difficult to perceive because they may be, accidentally, in the wrong type of job, (although I would argue that great leaders don't let accidents happen to their career). They might have a self-seeking and political boss who exploits their skills but takes care that the rest of the organization doesn't learn of the person's talents (but I would argue that a future leader would know how to ensure the rest of

> I would argue that great future leaders will always look comparatively great.

the organization finds out). The potential leader may be going through a fallow period, learning key skills before the next spurt of growth in ability (but I would argue that great future leaders will always look comparatively great). In other words, I concede that one cannot always see clearly who has the potential to become a great leader. As a consequence of my experience in organizing literally hundreds of leadership and management development programmes, and taking thousands of potential leaders through those programmes, I believe it is possible to predict who has and who does not have the gene of leadership.

If we look at the more general argument for the case that leaders are born, not made, the 20th century provides some evidence. We have seen more leadership and management development than ever before (look at the exponential growth of business schools) – but there has been little evidence that business school training itself has any effect on the rates of growth and decline of large organizations. There is a viable test, to prove the point. Consider the growth rates of businesses in the USA and the UK, where business schools mushroomed during the 30 years between 1960 and 1990, with very little consequent change in the national growth rates. Compare that to Japan and Germany, where there was almost no development of business school education but which had continuous, startlingly successful, growth rates. Interestingly, Japan is now indulging in the Western predilection for the creation of business schools for the training and development of some of its business executives. One wonders how soon this will have an effect and what it will be?

Global and major international corporations proliferate; but that requires fewer leaders, not more. Worldwide, there are also many more small to medium businesses. That may be a sign that an increasing number of people cannot abide the large corporate world; it may be indicative that modern technology facilitates the formation of more and smaller businesses. Yet it can also be taken as evidence that there are simply not enough great leaders around, so that we get more small and medium-sized businesses, because that is the size their leaders can cope with. Elliott Jaques has argued that organizations will grow to the size of the time horizon of their leader. I certainly agree although I would amend this to read that organizations will grow to the size of the leadership potential of their leader.

Organizations will grow to the size of the leadership potential of their leader.

Another observation, before closing the argument, is to notice that many leaders seem to get to the top without either training or management development. I remember my utter surprise upon learning that Sir Peter Thompson had risen to the leadership of the National Freight Consortium without any management or leadership training. He didn't need it because he knew instinctively how to lead and develop his own strategic vision. He is living proof of the argument that 'leaders are born, not made'.

Yet what about those many individuals who are in a leadership position now? Surely they are all leaders, by definition? I would argue that many of them are not leaders at all, merely holders of the position of leader. Andrew Kakabadse, a professor specializing in human resource studies at the Cranfield School of Management, has offered evidence that over 60 per cent of business organizations are badly managed. Worse, 52 per cent of chairmen and CEOs 'feel uncomfortable about the effectiveness of the top team leading the organization and the performance of its members' (Kakabadse 1991). In some ways, this is strong evidence that even those 'nominal leaders' know that they don't have what it takes. After all, Kakabadse's evidence is their own testimony about themselves!

What are the skills of these 'nominal leaders' who get into the top jobs but who were not born to be leaders? They have good political skills and are, almost without exception, highly driven individuals. Yet they lack essential leadership skills. When you examine their career patterns, although they have climbed to the top they have singularly failed to develop the traits of successful leadership, which are described below. It is often the case that others can see they are failing – but they can't.

When should you start your leadership career?

Most great leadership careers begin, unwittingly, during childhood. Psychometric research shows that frequently the drive to prove oneself, to climb to the top of a large organization can be laid at the doorstep of a highly ambitious mother who brings up her favoured, often only, child to want to please her so much that the child cannot stop trying, even when adult. Sometimes, just being an only child is enough to set off the sense of self-sufficiency and their 'need to achieve' (McClelland 1961) which is the hallmark of our classic leader. It may also stem from an accident of genetic inheritance such as naturally high-quality intellectual ability, character, charisma and (sometimes) mere physical height – there is some evidence that a statistically significant number of leaders are taller than average for their generation, without any corresponding proven correlation of size and brains.

In most cases, however, leadership potential and style of behaviour start at a very young age, although they are not always recognizable either as a precursor or a predictor of leadership. Some leaders display waywardness in their childhood. They sometimes lack concentration powers in the classroom. Some display a reluctance to settle down at university because they are so keen to get on with their leadership career. Bill Gates walked out of Harvard. Alan Sugar, possibly, might never have got in. Sometimes future leaders are so different from ordinary mortals that they are seen as 'difficult to manage' children, by those whose opinions count at this stage, such as school teachers and scout/guide troop leaders. Usually, however, their loving parents accept and understand that they are destined for greater things.

Some readers may already be feeling that they have not yet been included in any of the characteristics mentioned and are beginning to believe that they are not destined to be leaders. Patience! If you are willing to keep reading, it may be that those characteristics which mark *you* out as a leader of the future may be delineated later in the book.

WHAT ARE WE DEFINING AS SUCCESS?

Success, in the terms of this book, may be defined as making a substantial difference to an organization during one's occupation of the leadership position. This should be measured in terms of: economic results (profits); creating an increase in gainful and satisfying employment opportunities for the workforce; and making customers happy in the belief that they have achieved the best possible value for their expenditure on products and services. By contrast, imagine being the leader of a business where your customer service information tells you that most customers who use your products are either unhappy, unhealthy or otherwise angry about the product.

WHAT IS *EFFECTIVE* LEADERSHIP?

An effective leader is one who really makes things happen in his organization. He moves it along new paths. He makes it exciting to go to work because he makes sure the working day

What a great leader also does is to make the business succeed as a social entity.

will have structure and meaning, that the workforce understand what they are doing, why and to what purpose. He makes his shareholders and workforce rich and he makes his customers happy with the product. He also understands that organizations are more than just economic entities, realizing that, like any politician, social worker or life leader, he is running an organization that has more realities than just economic ones. He is a fertile 'imagineer' about the organization's future, (Peters 1992: 160–5), while understanding that when working hours for workers are increased, their families are deprived of their working parent or spouse. His decisions have as many social as economic implications. Recently I had to help a leader reduce the size of his organization from 6000 employees to 4500. It was the only way to save the whole business. He deliberately chose to let the people go early, in October, rather than hold them to their terms of contract and leave in December, while paying them for the full period, at considerable cost to the business. This ensured that they had the maximum chance of finding other employment (the October jobs market is infinitely superior to the December or January situation) and to ensure that their families suffered as little as possible during the Christmas holiday.

The effective leader takes decisions that make the organization succeed economically. What a great leader also does is to make the business succeed as a social entity. This leader wants people to feel proud to be working for the organization, as well as prosperous.

Why would effective leaders need help?

A question I am frequently asked is: 'If these guys are so good, how come they need you?' It's a rude question, but fair. My role is to offer a unique catalyzing skill which maximizes the leader's speed of development, thus allowing the potentially great leader to maximize his or her skills earlier than would otherwise be the case. Naturally, this begs the next important question. Why should any leader need somebody to help them lead or analyze what they must do? The answer relates to some of the conditions of the leadership situation, as well as some leadership qualities. The loneliness of leaders sometimes makes it desirable to use a confidant, such as myself (*see also* Chapter 3, below). Occasionally, some of them have crises of confidence – it helps to check that it's OK to do what they are doing. On one or two occasions, I have been called in to help them sort out particularly difficult political situations with their board of directors. In these situations, a go-between can be efficacious.

Let's examine a real example of just such a case.

Case study 1.1

EGOS, POLITICS AND POWER

A client had been the chief executive officer in an American business with revenues of about $10 billion per annum, and profits close to $2 billion. He himself earned about $3m p.a. and had to be considered to have had a highly successful career up to that time. Unfortunately, during the previous few years he had received a battering at the hands of the media and his achievements had been belittled. The situation had become so fraught that the company chairman had decided he could no longer continue in ▶

Fig. 1.1
THE STARTING AND FINISHING POSITIONS OF A GREAT LEADER
Starting position

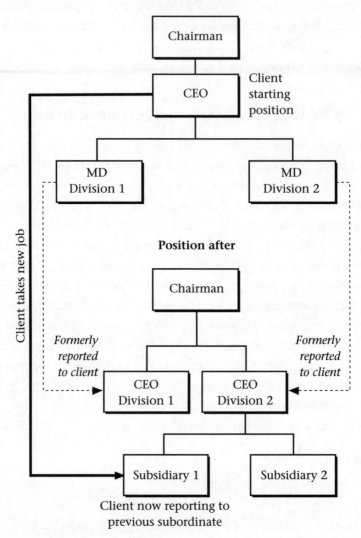

Client now reporting to
previous subordinate

The Client had risen to be the CEO of the parent corporation, in the USA. When I first met him, he had accepted a position reporting to the CEO of one of the two divisions his previous empire was sub-divided into.
To add to the difficulties of the situation, both his new boss and the boss of the other division had reported to him personally in his previous role.

the leadership role. It was beginning to affect both the share price and the perceived achievements of the chairman himself. Furthermore, some of the criticism could be considered justified, because he was considered to be weak when it came to taking tough decisions about people.

Consequently, the chairman offered my client the choice of leaving the corporation with a generous settlement or continuing his career with them but at a lower level in the business. He chose to move to a lower level. This was a sign, for me, of a truly great man. He had his ego so much under control that he could cope with everybody else thinking he was utterly defeated. To understand how bad his decision 'looked', *see* Figure 1.1.

As the Figure shows, my client had not only dropped in status from number two in the organization to one of several at the fourth level in the hierarchy, but he now reported to a person who previously had reported to him. Furthermore, another of his subordinates had taken over his previous job (and picked up all the long-term fruits of my client's excellent work). The client called me in because his boss, previously his subordinate, was trying both to humiliate him and also force him to resign, since the boss believed the media stories that my client was incompetent at both leadership and strategy. My client's instructions were to establish exactly what his boss thought, decide what was reasonable, help him decide how much and how little it would be appropriate to comply with, and then to devise a plan to neutralize the situation until he could prove that he was content with his new job, intended to do it well, was capable of loyalty and of accepting his new position and of doing it brilliantly, if given half a chance.

He then devised a plan which did just that. He had to decrease the size of his management team of 100 executives (not all reporting directly to him) to 50. He had to revise the strategy of his subsidiary and demonstrate within a year that he could make more profit than the parent division. He had to halve his overheads and to sacrifice his finance director who had made an important mistake in the previous year (and delivered a surprise shortfall of cash to the tune of $100 million).

He carried out the necessary action within one week and completed all the recommended changes within three months. He cut his costs from

$50m to $25m, halved his staff and doubled his cash flow and profits. Within a year, his position was so strong that he could be perceived to be more powerful than his boss. He was once more invited to attend all main board meetings and was seen as a key contender for succession to the chairman's position as the chairman began to plan for his own retirement. For me the key learning from him was that great leaders keep their egos firmly under control and their minds fixed on the longer term and the big picture. In addition, if he had not carried out the planned programme, there was a strong possibility that both he and his whole team would have been liquidated by his boss. That would also have resulted in the loss of the excellent profits he was to bring in for the parent corporation, within 12 months of the execution of his plan.

Who is the leader?

The ultimate leader is the person paid to take the biggest and most important decisions in his organization. Naturally, we also address all those people who aspire to become that type of leader. Great leaders spend their entire career learning how to be the best possible leader when they finally make it to the top. It is not possible to arrive in the ultimate leadership job and feel there is nothing else to learn. A leader is

> It is not possible to arrive in the ultimate leadership job and feel there is nothing else to learn.

always evolving, learning skills, developing traits and maturing the necessary characteristics of leadership. It is a characteristic of most successful people that they are always learning and are prepared to take their lessons from wherever they come.

In this book, I am usually referring to business organizations because that is where I have spent my career. These are the people I know best and it is their careers I can best describe. The advice I give is intended for them. Other leaders of other types of organization may find some or all of the contents of this book relevant to their own careers. I claim no expertise elsewhere. I know business life and I work with those senior corporate leaders. Most are people who don't make the newspaper headlines. (Later in the book I explain why wise leaders deliberately stay away from media limelight). In most organizations the person I am writing about is the president or the chairman. However, it could be the chief executive officer, chief operating officer, executive president, executive vice-president or managing director, in cases where the apparently more senior post is occupied by a non-executive chair or president.

Most of the corporations where I work and which are used as examples are large. The revenue of the organization may be measured in hundreds of millions or several billions of £s or $s. Employees are often numbered in thousands and tens of thousands. Often the profits are measured in hundreds of millions of £s or $s. Usually their customers are numbered in millions, rather than hundreds or thousands. Of course, I have worked with smaller organizations and found that most of the concepts are equally valid.

Some examples successful of leadership

Sir Winston Churchill had not been considered a great leader before World War Two, nor even a great politician. But during World War Two his oratory, his successful decisions and the Allies' eventual victory provide proof that, for the duration of the war, he was a great leader. This emphasizes that different situations require either different skills from the leader or different leaders. Interestingly, the common sense of the British public would not elect him as a postwar leader. Instead they voted for Clement Attlee, who was perceived as more likely to give the electorate the social justice that the country so badly needed.

Robert Goizueta led Coca-Cola for over a decade before he died in 1997. His belief in Coca-Cola was an obsession. He led it like a colonizing force, capturing global territory like an ancient conqueror. He increased the value of the company from $4.3 billion to $150 billion. Leaders like this, who encapsulate and transmit vision and belief, can add vast value to their business.

Richard Branson, founder and entrepreneurial leader of the Virgin group, has demonstrated that entrepreneurs can create and lead very large businesses, or large collections of businesses, as long as they make suitable arrangements for somebody else to run their large businesses in a corporate fashion. Branson achieves this by appointing clever, corporately skilled, managers to develop and grow the businesses, following his founding input. He then concentrates on helping them with the only corporate skill he really has in abundance, which is that of exploiting the media to achieve free publicity.

Sir Iain Vallance has successfully led British Telecom, a leading UK telecommunications corporation, without falling out with its regulator while still exploiting a high level of monopolistic profit potential. Although he has not yet succeeded in achieving his stated ambition of making BT into a global player, it must be one of the most profitable stories in the history of business leadership. The firm has made around £3 billion profit on revenues of between £12 and £13 billion for more than a decade (other than in 1993 when it downsized the business by so many thousands of people that redundancy costs stripped the profits for the year to just under £2 billion). Sir Iain has demonstrated steady, profit-led leadership, consistently maintaining high standards of integrity while ruthlessly pursuing maximum profits and manoeuvering the business into the potential to be a world player. In an industry with time horizons of ten to 20 years, it will be some time before we can really judge whether his leadership has been the great success it seems.

Sir Peter Thompson led the first privatization, during the prime ministership of Margaret Thatcher, of the then National Freight Consortium (later the NFC). He led it as a worker buyout, thus rendering thousands of ordinary truck and lorry drivers wealthy beyond their dreams, a value which fitted his personal beliefs. The business was bought from the government for just over £50 million. A few years later, still under his leadership, it was floated for considerably more than £1 billion. The business peaked in value at almost £2 billion. The important lesson here is that great leaders know their own Achilles heels – Sir Peter's powerful personality was such that many potential successors had trouble working in the shadow of his charismatic presence, leaving to find high level leadership roles in other corporations. NFC was left with a smaller pool of qualified people from which to choose his successor.

Examples of 'less successful' leadership

Peter Sherlock was brought in as CEO of the NFC by James Watson, who succeeded Sir Peter Thompson, as chairman. Sherlock was chosen by Watson in preference to an internal candidate, who was generally acknowledged by many people in the logistics and transportation industry to be exceptionally brilliant. At that time analysts in the City were saying that the NFC needed 'fresh blood', and was too insular, because it frequently appointed its leaders from within. Thus, what had been a virtue in earlier days became a sin. Peter Sherlock came complete with a full range of management jargon, but no understanding of either the industry or the NFC. This would not have been a problem had he been the *right* leader. Within weeks of his arrival at the NFC, Sherlock brought in a contingent of consultants from McKinsey, the strategy consultancy specialists. Two years later, and with substantial invoices for consultancy, the board decided to sack the imported whiz-kid. The lessons of failure that should be learned from this case are that no leader should pay undue attention to the City or to analysts, in preference to sound knowledge and informed opinion in one's own industry. Another key lesson is that the wrong CEO can take a business down to undreamed-of levels, even after a period of great success. During this CEO's two year occupancy of the leadership, the share price diminished rapidly; so did morale among the personnel of the business. Several years after his departure, NFC's business and share price have still not recovered.

Robert Allen was the boss of AT&T for more than ten years. He presided over a range of strategic initiatives which turned sour, such as entering the computer hardware and software manufacturing industries. However, he had the political skills to survive into retirement, in spite of apparently missing opportunities to exploit the company's inherited wealth and strategically strong position. The lesson here is that failing to take advantage of the business' basic strategic strengths and wasting corporate energy on the wrong initiatives may be equally damaging. AT&T is no longer the clear world leader it was at the beginning of his period in office; that must be perceived as 'less than maximum success'.

Robert Maxwell was the well-known entrepreneur who 'borrowed' the funds from his businesses' pension funds to prop up the value of the shares of his business, while using their value to both expand and to borrow more. He did this by exploiting an enormous and bullying personality, while gathering all the power into his own capacious hands. Everybody needs checks and balances, for their own sanity. In essence Maxwell appears to have had almost no moral precepts guiding his leadership of his business interests. The ultimate failure of his business career may serve as a demonstration of the need for moral fibre in a leader.

President Carter in the USA, was a skilled business person and thoroughly moral and sincere in every aspect of his life. However, as president his strengths became less useful. His sincerity and determination to behave honourably reduced his capacity to deal with dishonourable people, such as President Saddam Hussein on the hostages issues, because he was handicapped by a lack of insight into the actions of a leader who used a totally different moral code to his own. President Carter's earnest desire to do the right thing at all times may have led to an inability to respond with alacrity and the appropriate degree of ruthlessness when it was necessary. By most accounts his period in office was less than successful. The lesson here is that successful leadership in one domain of one's life may not translate into the ingredients for success in a different field.

Signs of leadership failure?

The first sign that a new leader is failing comes when you notice that their words and actions don't match. Their statements about the effects of strategic plans, usually made to City analysts and financial journalists, don't turn out as predicted. Quite soon they are heard blaming external causes, such as 'a strong currency'. It is interesting how nobody ever says, 'we did well this year, but only because the weak currency was in our favour'.

Another early syndrome of the failing leader is when they fail to get rid of the people who were in place before they arrived, who probably caused most of the problems in the first place. For example, if the City was right about the NFC needing to bring in new blood to freshen the leadership, at least one reason that the externally imported CEO failed was that, two years after his arrival, he had left all the previous incumbents in place. It was those leaders who had survived who organized the coup that forced the board to dismiss Peter Sherlock.

Any great leader should be able to change the quality of organization results within the first year of his leadership. There are many simple and justifiable ways of doing this which might be considered short term but which bring long term benefits. For example, it may be wise to institute a recruitment freeze.

> **It is interesting how nobody ever says, 'we did well this year, but only because the weak currency was in our favour'.**

This will control costs and may also be advisable because, until there has been time to consider the type of people needed, it may be better not to recruit at all. Similarly, all rebuilding work and buildings' extensions could be halted, until it is decided that these are the structures which will be necessary for the future of the business. It is always sensible to stop discretionary expenditure on PR and product development until a decision has been taken about what future products should be. These ideas seem tactical and short term. However, they achieve some long term advantages. First, they convince the board that the new leader knows what he is doing; that wins kudos and makes it easier to persuade them to accept any difficult, strategic advice that will be given at a later date. Second, it convinces the incumbent executive team that the newly installed leader really knows how to make a difference. Finally, it signals to all employees that the new person means business and gains their total attention. What I am suggesting is that there are so many formulae available to any competent leader that there should be no excuses for not improving the organization's results as soon as one assumes the leadership role. When leaders make excuses, rather than deliver results, even in their first year, it is a sign that they just do not have what it takes.

Another sign of a failing leader is that the jobs they have held prior to the final appointment begin to come apart at the edges and crumble. They often become increasingly political in their behaviour and actions, blaming other people and external events for the failure of the strategy. Failing leaders often then bring in a new CEO, chief operating officer or managing director, to implement the leader's strategic vision ('implementation is not my type of work'). In the same mode, they often call in McKinsey or some other strategy consultancy, to analyze at great cost what's wrong with the company and to develop a theory for change in the business.

Finally, you know the game is up when the newspapers regularly put 'troubled' in front of any articles about the organization. Simultaneously, the leader will start to look for the next job (usually by taking on too many non-executive directorships, hoping one will become the next job offer) when he/she should be concentrating on their own organization. The ultimate litmus test of failure will be that the leader starts to lay the blame on anybody else for the failure. He/she will also refuse to take responsibility for 'the organization's inability' to respond to his/her leadership.

WHAT ARE THE KEY INGREDIENTS OF A BUSINESS LEADER?

The leadership task range requires multifarious skills. Among the foremost are:

- tenacity
- stamina
- long term wisdom
- emotional intelligence
- judgement about what is worth fighting for (and what isn't)
- equanimity
- character
- capacity to inspire followership
- some form of generalized love for fellow human beings.

Throughout the book we will be elaborating on these qualities and offering explanations of how to improve when one might feel they need strengthening. Use the questionnaire opposite to measure yourself at this control point. Are you a future or present leader by the standards of this first list of requirements?

Questionnaire 1.2
A FIRST MEASURE OF LEADERSHIP SKILLS

Skill	Meaning	Self-applied score 1 (low) to 10 (high)
Tenacity	*Capacity for sticking to difficult-to-achieve tasks*	
Stamina	*Ability to stick at a job when the occasional career slow down takes place*	
Long term wisdom	*The ability to forecast the future of the industry, the development of one's colleagues and the probabilities of success of strategies*	
Emotional intelligence	*Having a range of insights which explain the personal motivations of people around you*	
Judgement about priorities	*Evaluating the business issues that are most likely to torpedo the business, if left unresolved*	
Equanimity	*The capacity to remain calm in the eye of the storm*	
Character	*Having values and beliefs that are sound and which guide you at all key decision points*	
Capacity to inspire followership	*Do people enjoy being led by you?*	
Love for fellow human beings	*Do you generally like people more frequently and more easily than you dislike them?*	
Add your total score		
Interpretation: Scores < 50 mean you need to develop more skills fast Scores > 70 mean you are well-grounded to evolve or be a leader Scores between 51 and 69 indicate a good base but needing development		

The key traits of leaders

I am defining *traits* as behaviours and styles that are accumulated as one learns to become a leader. They are differentiated from *skills* because they are acquired through diffusion, example, rather than learned in business schools or on development programmes. They are:

- the ability to get into leadership positions
- better quality judgement than any relevant peer group
- a capacity for survival (thick skin)
- ability to select effective subordinates
- ability to inspire 'ordinary' people to perform above par; inspiring followership
- making a profound enduring difference to the organization
- a deep sense of decency with moral fibre.

Let's examine each, in detail.

The ability to get into leadership positions

This is best observed in cases of people who gain a reputation for always being 'in the right place at the right time'. I compare it to the days when I ran a wholesale cash-and-carry business. About four times a year somebody would offer me a deal which, by the end of the year, proved to be worth about 50 per cent of the total year's profits. Furthermore, I only needed 50 per cent of each year to live most comfortably. So why didn't I just relax and do four deals a year? The answer was that if I were not running like a madman for the rest of the time, I could never be sure of being in the right place at the right time for just those four deals! The same goes for these leaders who are always just in the right place at the right time. It is not an accident; they move rapidly and create more opportunities to be in the right place at the right time.

Better quality judgement than any relevant peer group

The first manifestations are often at school. They stand out as leaders. They become the captain of the football or netball team. They get appointed as school captain. Above all, they are noticed early as having a form of maturity and judgement. The same qualities can be observed when they first go out to work. Without excessive deference, they are soon used by their boss to carry out important tasks. They are the first to be promoted because they become known for being a 'safe pair of hands'. It is their good judgement which is observed to be superior.

For those reading this book as a primer on what to do, think carefully about the paragraph above. In terms of most people, it means total and unceasing concentration from the start of their career, on using their best judgement all the time. It means rarely letting their feelings rule. It means always reflecting carefully before offering an opinion or carrying out any action at work. Is this what you do? If not, are you prepared to concentrate forever and do this? If you are, there is some consolation. Eventually it will become a habit and not feel so difficult or tiring. Furthermore, it may provide evidence that you may just have the necessary genetic strain.

A capacity for survival (thick skin)

One should not imagine that great leaders always avoid controversy or problems. Sometimes it is necessary to confront problems head on. They survive because they manage to get everybody to realize that they have made the right judgement and that difficult decisions have to be taken. The biggest decisions are usually the ones which require

> A great leader does not confront people with a decision but persuades and debates the issue, until people understand.

the thickest skin. Making the larger investment decisions, or deciding to put the corporation up for sale, or moving into or out of major markets, are the types of decisions which cause the greatest angst to leaders and their followers. The mark of a great leader is that they realize it is necessary to get people to understand why they see the final decision taken as being the very best in the circumstances. A great leader does not confront people with a decision but persuades and debates the issue, until people understand. They realize that confrontation is unlikely to bring others around. They explain for as long and as hard as is necessary.

Ability to select effective subordinates

Having to dismiss a friend who has become ineffective or who is manifesting characteristics which are detrimental to the organization is often the hardest type of decision a leader may have to take. It is one of the worst forms of leadership failure when the leader does nor confront these problems. Making the right decisions about people often requires a special combination of intuition and experience. The great leader usually has an intuition about who could fit a particular job and when the person will be ready for it. A feel for people and their development cycle and innate capacity becomes a sixth sense. Wise leaders back up their instincts by sharing responsibility with skilled human resource managers, interviewing individually and in teams, and psychometric testing. When they can, they appoint people for trial periods to ensure they can be returned to the positions where they were effective previously, if they fail in their new appointment.

Failing to organize quality succession, which then destroys what you have built, is not good long term leadership.

Ability to inspire ordinary people to perform above par: inspiring followership

By definition, the world consists mainly of 'ordinary' people of average ability. Ultimately, every large organization, and the skills of the people in it, regress towards the mean. In those circumstances, how do great leaders make their people perform better than anybody else? They have to, because one cannot always have a consistently better strategy or superior products than every competitor. Great leaders do it by the quality of *inspiration*. They are able to make people want to perform better. The exemplar of the contrary is the teacher who tells a child not to expect to do well in its exams; this is a proven method to ensure the child's failure. The opposite applies for great leaders. They make people want to perform above themselves. They show them how to be better. This skill is closely aligned with the ability of good leaders to attract followers. Getting people to follow, and want to follow, is a prime leadership skill. It results from a combination of charisma, persuasiveness and sheer determination.

Making a profound enduring difference to the organization

This particular trait can often only be recognized *post hoc*, when the leader has left the organization or department. My favourite example of this quality was a splendid leader I worked with in the transport industry. When I started working with this man, I visited the various divisions and districts he had worked in over the past 15 years. Astonishingly, people who had not worked with him for ten years or more still spoke of him with awe and affection. All his employees still spoke of the qualities he emphasized. For example, he always emphasized cash collection, often achieving reductions in outstanding debt of over 50 per cent. They still carried out the same procedures in the regions where he had been. In one area I came across a secretary who had worked for him more than ten years before. She told me that 'he had been the most brilliant leader. It had always been obvious.' I asked if she ever saw him (ten years later he was responsible for all the overseas businesses and was often abroad). She replied that she received a handwritten letter from him every Christmas telling her what he had been up to during that year and giving her all his news. I suspect that woman lived for those letters. Apparently he told nobody, so did not do it to boast about how to behave. He just did it! I suspect he wrote them, as would many quality leaders, with a whole range of agendas. First, they were a genuinely kind thing to do for an employee from the past. Second, they forced him to review his own progress, as seen through the eyes of an ordinary employee. Third, they reminded him of the many thousands of employees it takes to make a large corporation tick. Finally, it reminded him of his humanity and his roots. To know where he was going to, he needed to remember where he had come from.

A profound sense of decency with moral fibre

If I had listed all the traits above, without this final, key one, of decency and moral fibre, I could have been describing Hitler, Mussolini or, indeed, some of the failures listed earlier, such as Robert Maxwell. Many leaders, who must be considered to have failed, still leave massive achievements behind them. But if they do not have this sense of decency and moral fibre, they can be as great a menace as they are an important leader. Maxwell had great skills, but he left behind thousands of people, who had given him their loyalty at work, without the pensions they had counted upon to enjoy their well-deserved retirement. Those football club managers who take 'bungs' (personal payments) as an extra cost to the selling club when they buy players, never see themselves as lacking moral fibre. But their 'premiums' are extra costs that are extracted at the cost of their clubs, other footballers and the paying public. Taking the money shows a lack of moral fibre. It is strange how few of them realize this. President Suharto of Indonesia has created an appalling system of nepotism, bribery and corruption. It has led to a systemic failure of the otherwise inspirational economic leadership he has provided, for over three decades, in the fourth largest nation in the world (by population). Ultimately, his lack of moral fibre and the subsequent inability of his family and himself to control their greed and set standards for others, has led to so many false indicators in the system of transactions throughout his country, that nobody can now do business under proper conditions of economic analysis.

How can the leader know that he is ineffective and stop himself?

An obvious first requirement of a leader is a ruthless honesty with himself. This is a truly rare quality in most failing leaders (and even in some successful ones). But, if one can do it, one should look for the following signals that one is failing:

- if you really cannot see where the short- or long-term profitability will be coming from
- if you feel overwhelmed *after* the first three months in the job (it is normal to feel overwhelmed *during* the first three months)
- when you start to feel that your subordinate(s) could certainly do the job better than you
- when you feel continuously tired and depressed
- when you long for holidays for the first time in your career
- when you start to think more about past triumphs than future achievements
- when your spouse starts to remind you that you really don't need the money
- when you know you are sitting in the board room hoping that nobody will realize that you don't have a clue what to do next (they always do realize!).

LEADERSHIP IN POLITICS: SIMILARITIES TO AND DIFFERENCES FROM BUSINESS

The question often arises whether the nation would benefit from being run by business leaders rather than politicians. Some people believe that the skills needed to head an important business are much more complex than the skills needed to run a government department. *Ergo*, business leaders should be able to do the job of government easily and more effectively! Let's examine some recent 'classical' political leaders and see how they match up to the corporate skills set. If we use examples that everybody would recognize as leaders such as Winston Churchill, John Major, Tony Blair, John F. Kennedy and William Hague we should be able to note the differences better and make one or two predictions as well. Table 1.1 illustrates this.

> **The question often arises whether the nation would benefit from being run by business leaders rather than politicians.**

Table 1.1 Measuring political leaders against corporate skill sets

The key leadership skills	Political leaders				
	Winston Churchill	John Major	Tony Blair	John F. Kennedy	William Hague
The ability to get into leadership positions	Yes	Yes	Yes	Yes	Yes
Better quality judgement than any relevant peer group	Yes	No	Yes	No	No
A capacity for survival (thick skin)	Yes	Yes	Yes (?)	Yes	No
Ability to select effective subordinates	Yes	No	?	No (?)	No
Ability to inspire others to perform above par; inspiring followership	Yes	No	Maybe	Yes	No?
Making a profound enduring difference to the organization	Yes	No	Maybe	No	Can't tell yet
A profound sense of decency with moral fibre	No	Yes	Can't tell yet*	No	Can't tell yet*
Employable as business leader?	**Yes**	**No**	**Maybe**	**No**	**Maybe**

*Neither has been in a leadership position for a long enough period of time to make value judgements about their skills in this category.

Of course, my table may be questioned in terms of judgement about some of the individuals in some areas. However, by and large, the judgments are reasonably middle of the road on each of the key skill leadership areas. It is obvious that, on most criteria, the majority of people who succeed in getting to the top of the greasy pole of politics, would almost certainly never make it in the corporate world .

Does the contrary apply? The evidence would suggest that corporate leaders find it equally difficult to make the transition into the political world. In part this may be explained by the possibility that both need such long apprenticeships that if one does not start young in either, there just isn't time to become proficient enough to become successful as a political leader after a corporate career and as a corporate leader after a successful political career.

So, what are the differences between political and corporate leadership?

Table 1.2 sets out my view of the similarities and differences between the role of leadership in business compared to politics. My guess is that representatives from both the political and corporate sides could object to my definitions of what makes successful leadership in the other side. But the litmus test must surely be how few politicians or business leaders manage to achieve successful careers in the others' territory. For politicians, the main attribute they seem to be able to offer is their range of contacts in Whitehall or their particular experience of legislation they have themselves played a part in enacting. For business leaders, what they seem mainly to be able to offer is efficiency, measured by the dubious quantifiers of 'cost benefit analysis'. The simple conclusion is that the ranges of leadership skills in the political and corporate worlds are so different from each other that it is almost impossible to make the transfer. Another explanation is provided by an examination of the measuring tools of success in each of their professions. In business, success is measured by the relatively objective criterion (in the long run) of profits; in politics, there is the equally objective measure of votes at elections, which, in turn, confer power. These criteria of accomplishment are very different in nature and it takes entirely different skills and processes to achieve consistent success. Another key difference between business leaders and political leaders is their time horizons. Corporate leaders must balance the needs of all their stakeholders to arrive at the optimal time horizon for the business, given its markets and the time it takes to develop the necessary infrastructure to supply that market. Political leaders are constrained by ever-decreasing time horizons as their next election approaches. Harold Wilson's famous political dictum that 'a week is a long time in politics' is increasingly true for politicians as elections draw near. They are therefore forced to take decisions on the basis of the electorate's capacity to accept the consequences, rather than because it is what is best for the economy or any particular section of the community (unless it carries enough votes to get them re-elected).

Table 1.2 Measuring political leaders' skills against corporate skills

The key corporate leadership skills	The key political leadership skills
The ability to get into leadership positions	The ability to get into leadership positions
Better quality judgement than any relevant peer group	Ability to impress a peer group with personality and brains to create a caucus, thus forcing the leader to offer posts when the party finally achieves power
A capacity for survival (thick skin)	A capacity for survival (very thick skin)
Ability to select effective subordinates	Ability to make the best of the subordinates one is obliged to use
Ability to inspire ordinary people to perform above par, inspiring fellowship	Ability to survive, once in office, and wait for the rare opportunity to fight for the final leadership role
Making a profound enduring difference to the organization, measurable by profits	Only history decides in the long run. No objective criteria (profits) exist. Short-run criterion is successful re-election
A profound sense of decency with moral fibre	Appearance of profound decency with a capacity to suspend it with alacrity for the purposes of survival
Usable as a politician?	**Employable as business leader?**

THE TRAITS OF SUCCESSFUL LEADERSHIP

On the understanding that traits are best understood as acquired habits or an accumulation of symptoms that can be observed, one can test whether a manager is successfully developing the habits and craft of great leadership. Everything successful leaders do, and every post they pass through, remains successful long after they go away. Their work achievements have much more permanence than the temporary patching-up jobs that lesser managers use to achieve their next promotion. Successful leaders are nearly always promoted early – but they still complete their current task before moving on to the new one. They rarely need to be looking for promotion because it always seems to come to them. They are never arrogant and frequently humble. They usually have full lives, giving attention to their family, playing sports, following hobbies and other pursuits. Their rounded lives are rarely defined only by the leadership job they do. They measure their success in life by their own standards of happiness and well-being, rather than other peoples' perceptions of their 'successful career'. Part of the success of their career is underpinned by the way they value having a full life more than just achieving a successful career.

> **Successful leaders are nearly always promoted early – but they still complete their current task before moving on to the new one.**

How and why bad leaders and idiots get to the top

First, the poor leader invariably learns the tricks of getting promoted early in their career. As we have already seen (Kakabadse 1991), there are a lot of poor managers with defective judgement. Such people promote fools like themselves continuously, partly because they do not know any better; because they have poor judgement; and, also, because talented people frighten and intimidate them. Nominal Leaders learn when young how to win political games and claim credit for the work of others. Sometimes they have even been better than average performers for a period in their career; see Jaques' (1982) theory of time spans of discretion to understand how some people can get to a certain level where their development stops. Once they are at the top, it is very hard to remove them because by the time these nominal leaders attain power, they know all the political tricks of how to stay there. Once idiots get into senior positions, the inordinate difficulties of removing them from positions of control often conspire to keep them there.

The prime skill of nominal leaders is that they learn to look good. They may have even performed well for some part of their career. They will, almost certainly, know the right people in the right places. Physically, they are often quite tall, causing them to get noticed more easily. Nominal leaders are usually aggressive, immensely ambitious and driven individuals. Occasionally one finds they are intellectual and well-qualified with degrees, and the odd MBA, which gives them a vocabulary and appearance of understanding, without the necessary accompanying insights. Above all, their greatest skill is in managing their own career rather than the organizations they damage!

How do individuals know they have the qualities of leadership?

Most individual leaders feel a sense of destiny, they feel driven to lead rather than follow. They can see clearly when those who are meant to be leading are making mistakes – and they work out how to help them lead better rather than make them look foolish. They are often appointed the leader of school teams, captain of their school, or elected to represent their fellow undergraduates at university.

When they start their first job, other leaders at work choose to be their mentor. They always have a deep involvement in their work, whilst retaining control over an important part of themselves that remains uninvolved. Their early tasks may have relatively short completion periods, yet they will conceptualize their role in a context of between one and five years. They are always ready for the next job because they see how to do it better than the person currently doing it (without wishing anyone to be demoted).

Do they know they have the gene? Most, when asked frankly and in confidence, answer that they always knew they were destined for a leadership role; they just did not know how and when it would come. Many have had some form of setback during their career, but they always continued to drive forward because of this inner sense that they were going to make it to the top, somewhere.

How do others know a person is destined to be a leader?

Naturally gifted leaders seem to command respect without resorting to tricks. They are always able to offer quality judgments and insights in response to an enquiry. Remaining calm, they tend to focus on objective truths rather than get sidetracked or involved in self-evidently subjective opinions. They appear to 'command space' whenever they are in a meeting. They exude profound character and people defer to them naturally, rather than them needing to capture attention. Above all, people want to follow them and seem to enjoy being led by them.

Situational leadership

Situational leadership is a concept which was developed originally by Hersey and Blanchard (1977), in their successful book, *Management of Organizational Behaviour: Utilizing Human Resources*. It describes the need for leaders to adapt their leadership style to the situation they find themselves in, as a consequence of the business' needs or the type of people they have working for them. No leader will be competent in every type of situation.

I would take this concept a little further, observing that some particular types of corporate situation are better suited to specific leadership styles. I further suggest that it is almost inconceivable that any single leader will be able to master all the potential styles (my list is both different and wider ranging than that of Hersey and Blanchard) in the varied situations (start-up, high growth, maturity, post-growth and liquidation) that businesses go through in the course of an industry life cycle which may endure anywhere between a few months (a microchip for a computer) and 200 years (the telecommunications industry).

A categorization of types of leader

Leadership styles can be categorized as in the following table. The descriptions are not always flattering, but this is meant to be reflective of reality rather than ideals and each style can be just as valid a leadership trait as any other. All these types are those that can be found successfully leading large businesses.

Table 1.3 Leadership styles and their descriptions

	Leadership style	Description
1	Egocentric	Self-centred, dominant, runs the empire from the centre
2	Autocratic	Sends the answers down from the top, non-consultative
3	Superior egalitarian (*primus inter pares*)	Participative but always giving impression of knowing the answers, makes people feel superior and worthy
4	Conflictual	Uses conflict, anger and strife to inspire and annoy people towards success
5	Team builder	Mollycoddles and develops teams until they achieve superior results just by wanting to please the leader
6	Strategic	Always communicating the vision and the path forwards, focused and uncomplicated, reputed for big-picture clarity
7	The people person	An extraordinary person who appears, on the surface, to be ordinary yet makes everybody around feel extraordinary
8	The politician	Always balancing and manipulating the stakeholders to keep the power nexus balanced and controlled at the centre

A categorization of situations requiring different types of leader

There are only a limited number of situations which a leader can normally find him or herself in. The following is not necessarily a comprehensive, list.

   If we place these two sets of classification of both types of leader and situations in which businesses need the leader's skills, we will be able to deduce which styles are most and which least relevant to the range of situations leaders might find themselves in. It can also be used to reflect under which circumstances good leaders may appear to be poor leaders.

Table 1.4 Leader types and their descriptions

Situation	Meaning
Entrepreneurial	Business in start up or strong growth phases under leadership of original founder
Corporate	Large quoted business, mixture of mature and (possibly) growth products
Turn round	Sick, mature business with declining demand and/or a cost structure which renders it unable to compete in its market
Steady state	Mature business, requiring application of steady management of mature, profitable market
Rapid growth	Immature market requiring clever development of brands in growth markets, possibly with high innovation
Consolidation	Business at close of rapid growth, requiring transition from rapid growth to steady state
Slimming following rapid growth	Business at close of rapid growth requiring rapid transition to steady state because overheads have built so rapidly, they could break the business
Fattening following excessive slimming	Business which has been excessively downsized requiring rebuilding to avoid dying from lack of human resources
Move from product to customer focus	Business at close of new market development rapid growth led by product innovation requiring transition to mature market by locking customers into brand awareness
Move from market share to cost control	Business at close of new market development rapid growth led by product innovation requiring transition to mature market by controlling costs to win mature market fight on price

Table 1.5 Comparison between leadership styles and business situations

Business situation	Leadership style							
	Ego-centric	Auto-cratic	Superior	Conflictual	Team builder	Strategic	People person	Politician
Entrepreneurial	Fit	Fit	Rarely	Fit	Neutral	Rarely	Fit	Rarely
Corporate	Fit	Fit	Fit	Rarely	Fit	Fit	Fit	Fit
Turn-round specialist	Fit	Fit	Fit	Fit	Rarely	Rarely	Rarely	Fit
Rapid growth	Fit	Fit	Rarely	Fit	Rarely	Tactics	Fit	Neutral
Consolidation	Rarely	Rarely	Fit	Rarely	Fit	Fit	Fit	Fit
Slimming following rapid growth	Rarely	Fit	Rarely	Fit	Rarely	Fit	Tactics	Fit
Fattening following excessive slimming	Rarely	Rarely	Neutral	Rarely	Fit	Fit	Fit	Neutral
Move from product to customer focus	Rarely	Rarely	Fit	Rarely	Fit	Fit	Fit	Fit
Move from market share to cost control	Fit	Fit	Fit	Fit	Neutral	Fit	Neutral	Neutral

An examination of the matrix in Table 1.5 demonstrates some interesting insights. Firstly, the most valuable leadership styles are the autocratic and the people person. This is an apparent contradiction since the two styles are at opposite ends of the stratum. However, because all good leaders choose their style for effectiveness this merely informs us that there are more situations which require these styles than others. If one considers some examples, the verisimilitude and usefulness of the layout becomes quite clear. Think of Alan Sugar. He obviously has leadership skills but they are not of the usual corporate mode. His two most self-evident styles are 'Egocentric' and 'Conflictual'. As we see, those styles suit the entrepreneurial and rapid growth scenarios which are the phases of his business career which have been most successful. Consider the example of Lord Sterling, the long-term leader of P&O, the transport, shipping, housebuilding and industrial conglomerate. His two most self-evident styles are 'Autocratic' and 'Superior'. One of the prevalent situations in his empire is the need for consolidation (in those mature, P&O businesses such as house building and transport). The model would predict that his 'Autocratic' style would fail in the consolidation businesses. This explains why Lord Sterling has been criticised in the press for his handling of those businesses when calls were made for his resignation. Other businesses he runs are in a condition of moving from product to market focus. An example would be the cross-Channel ferry business, which, following the opening of the Channel Tunnel, has had to become much more market- and customer-oriented than before. Lord Sterling's 'Autocratic' and 'Superior' styles are both fits for this type of business situation. Subsequently, he has received strong praise, both in the media and from other commentators for his handling of these businesses, and has defused earlier criticism of any shortcomings.

Interestingly, given the range of different situations examined, the least useful style for a leader appears to be that of team builder. This also appears to conflict with the pervasive theory of the last decade or two during which team building was continuously recommended by management gurus. The relevant point to note is that leaders may *need* teams to deliver their vision – but if they employ a team-building style, they may be less effective. An example of this, from my own files, is the leader I worked with who had taken a run-down group of distribution businesses and developed a highly profitable, £150 million per annum business, which gained a national reputation of being customer-oriented in the goods distribution industry. It also achieved high profit levels. The industry was thus in a state of consolidation. He was the best team builder I ever knew. He was so good at building teams that we often commented that he took weaklings and made them strong, through the strength of the teams he built around himself and them. He also had the most intense loyalty to his team. He never got rid of anybody, even when they had proved to be almost, congenitally stupid. A few years after this success, he was asked to lead another division, in the office and house removals industry, which was going through a tough retrenchment period, suffering from industrial recession and low levels of house sales (therefore, less demand for household goods removals). The industry was thus in a state of moving from market share to cost control. His skills as a team builder went from being a good fit to neutral. His high-flying career slowed down and he never regained momentum.

Careful study of Table 1.5 also shows that the Egocentric and Conflictual styles are the two which are most often the best fit, in most business situations. Upon reflection, this is not surprising. The definition of both, even though they are encountered only too frequently throughout British industry, contradict most peoples' ideas about what leadership is meant to be. But they are both useful, for different reasons. The Egocentric style runs things from the centre. It is dominant and self-centred, but it is also economical in the use of the leader's time, effective in not tolerating unnecessary discussion and debate (as long as the leader is nearly always right) and, in situations of start-up, growth or rapid change, when there is no time for debate, it is highly appropriate. Likewise, the Conflictual style. It suits best all situations of change, which are stressful and require the creation and loosening of ideas and energy. The Conflictual style achieves this effectively. Of course, the Conflictual style exacts a high price on everybody involved: it increases stress and burn-out; it wastes some excellent potential leaders, who cannot cope with other leaders who use that style; and it often wears out, prematurely, the leader themselves.

Finally, the situation which requires the least skill appears to be that of fattening the organization following slimming. A quick glance at the demands of such a situation will confirm this accords with common sense and the poor achievements of so many leaders in this situation. Examples abound in many monopoly industries in the UK and USA. In essence, this situation consists of taking a company making large profits and spending the profits until the excess organizational slack is expended. Most competent managers can do that relatively easily.

SITUATIONAL LEADERSHIP

Some great careers have been built through having the right leader in the right place, in exactly the type of situation his skills, style and career were getting him ready for. We have said that this is true of Winston Churchill. It also helps to explain the success of Sir Alastair Morton, a fine exponent of the Conflictual style, who was exactly the right person to deliver an economically impossible task, with monumental financing and building difficulties in a rapid growth situation. It helps to explain why, what looked from the outside like an appalling piece of leadership, was actually an opportune meeting of the right man for the right job at exactly the right time. It was certainly worth a knighthood!

RECOMMENDED READING FOR CHAPTER 1

Adair, J. (1988) *Effective Leadership*. London: Pan.

Blake, R. R. and Mouton, J. S. (1964) *The New Managerial Grid*. Houston: Gulf.

Covey, S. R. (1989) *The 7 Habits of Highly Effective People*. New York: Simon & Schuster.

Cox, D. L. (1993) *Management Fleas & Leadership Flies*. Burton-on-Trent and Derby: Tresises.

Crainer, S. (1996) *Key Management Ideas*. London: Pitman Publishing.

Hamel, G. and Prahalad, C. K. (1994) *Competing for the Future*. Boston, MA: Harvard Business School Press.

Hersey, P. and Blanchard K. H. (1977) *Management of Organizational Behaviour: Utilizing Human Resources*, 3rd edn. Engelwood Cliffs, NJ: Prentice-Hall.

Hickson, D. J. *et al.* (1986) *Top Decisions*. Oxford: Basil Blackwell.

Jaques, E. (1976) *A General Theory of Bureaucracy*. London: Heinemann.

Jaques, E. (1982a) *The Form of Time*. London: Heinemann.

Jaques, E. (1982b) *Free Enterprise, Fair Employment*. London: Heinemann.

Kakabadse, A. (1991) *The Wealth Creators*. London: Kogan Page.

Koch, R. and Campbell, A. (1994) *Wake Up and Shake Your Company*. London: Pitman Publishing.

Levicki, C. J. (1996) *The Strategy Workout*. London: Financial Times Pitman Publishing.

Lewis, R. and Lowe, P. (1992) *Individual Excellence*. London: Kogan Page.

McClelland, D. (1961) *The Achieving Society*. Princeton, NJ: Van Nostrand.

Peters, T. (1992) *Liberation Management*. London: Macmillan.

White, R.P., Hodgson, P. and Crainer, S. (1996) *The Future of Leadership*. London: Pitman Publishing.

Biographies of companies and leaders

Bramson, A. (1990) *Pure Luck*. Wellingborough: Patrick Stephens.

Davies, H. (1981) *The Grades*. London: Weidenfeld & Nicolson.

Heller, R. (1993) *The Super Chiefs*. New York: Truman Talley/Plume.

McLachlan, S. (1983) *The National Freight Buy-Out*. London: Macmillan.

Morita, A. (1994) *Made in Japan*. London: HarperCollins.

Sloan, A. P. (1965) *My Years with General Motors*. New York: MacFadden-Bartell.

Thompson, P. (1990) *Sharing the Success*. London: Fontana.

Walton, S. (1993) *Made in America*. New York: Bantam.

A LEADER IS ALWAYS LEADING, WHATEVER THE JOB

....

This chapter develops the theme that great

leadership careers are managed from

the beginning. Great leaders are always

perfecting their leadership skills. They make

any job a leadership role in the organization. A

leader should always consider themselves to be

in training for their ultimate leadership role.

The ultimate leadership job title can be

anything from President, Senior VP, Executive

VP, Chair, CEO, or MD.

....

POTENTIAL LEADERS PREPARE THEMSELVES FOR THEIR ULTIMATE CAREER GOALS

It is important to get a sense of destiny early in a career and try to behave in a manner which is at all times appropriate to the role of being a leader. It is often remarked that good leaders seem to be 'mature for their age'. What is that maturity composed of? Maturity can be defined by a person seeing the *larger-scale* and *longer-term* consequences of their actions more clearly than their peer group. Throughout their career great leaders always have a part of themselves that is *helicoptered* (Chapter 5) above the action, observing it dispassionately from above. They reflect carefully and try never to behave in a way that could leave damage in their wake and might act as a hostage to fortune later in their careers.

Does this mean that they are timid people, or excessively calculating? No. It means that all their key decisions are taken in perspective. They co-ordinate their overall need to use their brains, expend their energy, and give reign to their personalities. They keep everything in perspective. These people's capacity for leading balanced lives requires great concentration and more care than most people are prepared to give to their careers. Although they are

> **Wise leaders are extremely prudent in choosing the right partner/spouse to share their success in life.**

endowed with more potential than the average, these people sometimes claim it is not an endowment but a curse because it can never be switched off. Like some academics, once their machine is switched on, it has to stay that way. That can be a lifelong pleasure or a curse!

There is one area I would single out as being of crucial importance. A leader's choice of partner is extremely sensitive. The wrong partner can not only damage a career but make the rewards of a successful career not worth having, because there is nobody one wants to share them with. Controversially, I would assert that wise leaders are extremely prudent in choosing the right partner/spouse to share their success in life. How do they do this? I don't think they get involved with people they don't love. Rather, *they are careful about who they allow themselves to fall in love with*.

In contrast, it is remarkable that many failed leaders that one meets seem to be allied with the wrong partner. For people who care to use their life skills and energies to the maximum, choosing the wrong partner can be a heavy weight upon their career (not to speak of their personal happiness). For those readers who are in this situation, one has to assume that you are probably so good at leadership that you know how to overcome the problems of managing a life with somebody who is likely to cause both them, and you, grief on a continuing basis. You know you have the spare energy that goes into coping with the emotional incidents that regularly occur. It may be a pity you didn't fall in love with somebody else, but you are prepared to live with the price of your love.

Usually, good leaders run an emotionally balanced life with time for family and hobbies. They keep their body as well as their mind fit and don't become entrapped by an excessive love of luxury. This ensures they are rarely obliged to take career decisions for money rather than for intellectual excitement or the fun of the challenge. They have hobbies, not only because they enjoy them, but also because they need distraction from the grind of corporate and business life, which can be, occasionally, quite arid in its subject matter. The corporate world, unfortunately, also contains some of the world's greatest philistines and bores. Leaders who may have developed sophisticated tastes need to have interests outside of their businesses, to keep alive their spirit of curiosity, intellectual craving and need for aesthetic beauty.

Please note that I am not intending to insult ordinary workers or managers. But leaders, by their nature, tend to be single-minded in their pursuit of a career. They need their career because it probably gives them the only suitable unique outlet for their energy and brain power. Other workers often have less energy and range than a 'classical' leader, which means they may need to devote more time to their career or to their private life. Occasionally, one forms the impression that somebody appears to have tremendous leadership potential, because they display a great capacity for intellectual and aesthetic pleasures and pursuits. This may be why they choose not to pursue their potential in terms of leadership skills. One often finds they place less emphasis on their career, based upon their disinclination to become over-focused on it. However, it remains true that they probably have less genuine leadership ability in spite of their possibly healthier and more rounded view of priorities in their personal lives.

Of course, successful leaders also have private lives. They don't fool themselves that their business friends are their true friends and their business life is really also their private life. They don't make the mistake of using the corporate hospitality tent as their preferred socializing tool. They know their private life is meant to be *private*. They respect their personal friends and their time with them and tend to keep their social and their business lives separate. It is almost always a disappointment for a leader or individual when business associates cross the boundary to personal friendship. Why? Because the leader will never be able to tell if they are only good at appearing to be a friend and are not a sincere intimate at all. Secondly, the incentive to appear sincere is much stronger in business relationships. A sincere business friend may well turn out to be a shallow personal friend – there is less to motivate them to behave befittingly. Without the business interest in common, you often find there is nothing else to cement the friendship.

One usually finds that highly competent leaders also have enough social skills to find, at least as many private friends as they need, to have an interesting social life. Overall, the life of most successful leaders can be most easily summarized as 'a life in equilibrium'.

The above is not to intended to paint a false picture that great leaders lead idyllic lives with no clouds on the horizon, no family troubles, perfect marriages and children who grow up to be perfectly amenable. Leaders, being human, are subject to the normal travails and problems of life. Nobody can avoid the problems that we are all vulnerable to. It is how people handle their problems that makes the difference. Leaders get divorced because their marriages break up, like anybody else. Leaders also have children who get into trouble with drugs and other adolescent problems, as so many do. Some find their sexual preferences are not in harmony with common practice. They learn to cope, as every other person has to cope. They manage their lives. They deal with the problems. And, hopefully, they survive and triumph, as do most other people, when confronted with the real world of normal troubles.

Leaders control the processes of their leadership career at every stage

Most leaders that I have worked with, at first made statements like 'I did not expect to become a top leader. Promotions just kept coming'. However, when one gets to know them better, they admit that they *had* always felt they would get to the top of any organization with which they were associated. Various authors and academics have pondered this question, which goes directly to the heart of the question, 'is there a leadership gene?' I refer elsewhere to McClelland's (1961) work on the *need to achieve* which drives so many people, at every level of work. Elliott Jaques (1976, 1982a, 1982b) is another eminent academic who has developed many theories and tools of analysis about human beings' capacity for work. These theories help to explain some of the phenomena being examined.

Jaques developed a theory of *time spans of discretion*. This describes how different employees feel able to cope with their responsibilities, for varying lengths of time, before needing supervision or the comfort of encouragement from a supervisor. Jaques developed these concepts into a predictive theory of *individuals' personal developmental stages in maturation of capacity* (Jaques 1976: 165–6). In my own research, I rename Jaques' *individuals' personal developmental stages in maturation of capacity* as *time horizons*, for the sake of simplicity and comprehension. Jaques developed tools of measurement whereby he believed he could predict the level of skill a person would evolve to, and how rapidly, over the course of their career. He also found that some leaders have time horizons spanning different periods of time. The longer the time horizon of the leader, the larger the organization they could successfully lead. An individual's final career capacity for decision making was called their time-horizon stratum. Jaques '[came] to the conclusion that the array of time-span progression curves expresses a fundamental regularity in the patterns of growth of competence in adults, as measured by the time frame – the maximum time-span of intention which the individual can muster in working activities, that is to say, goal-directed activities' (Jaques 1982a: 151). These strata can be defined in terms of the following periods of time (over which the person was capable of taking decisions on behalf of the organization):

Table 2.1 Elliott Jaques' discrete time-stratum periods

Stratum 1	0–3 months
Stratum 2	3–12 months
Stratum 3	1–2 years
Stratum 4	2–5 years
Stratum 5	5–10 years

A person can reach his or her stratum peak, or maximum work and skill capacity, at any age. Plainly, most reach it in their more mature years. One obvious danger with Jaques' theory is the general belief that it is better to have a long stratum, because people think it makes them appear cleverer. Thus they are tempted to exaggerate the evidence which helps place them in their appropriate stratum. Jaques always advised me to sort out false claims by asking people what concrete steps they have taken to implement the objectives of their longest time horizon, which is my equivalent test of a person's stratum. I used this trial on the leader of a major subsidiary of a major oil corporation. He had tried to impress me with the length of his time horizon by describing the minerals, unknown and unnamed, which his business was going to explore for and extract, in previously unfathomed depths of land and sea, for use in, as yet, undeveloped industries. I asked him what he or the business had actually done to further this amazing vision. The answer was 'nothing so far'. Ultimately, his time horizon was closer to a stratum 3 (1–2 years) than the stratum 5 he was claiming. People destined to have leadership careers probably understand intuitively many of the theories being described here. It is important for such people to manage themselves carefully, knowing when they should be advancing their career towards their ultimate destination and when they should be biding their time, learning fresh skills and waiting for the next spurt in their leadership development.

Fig. 2.1 ELLIOTT JAQUES' THEORY OF TIME HORIZONS AND PERSONAL DEVELOPMENT OVER TIME

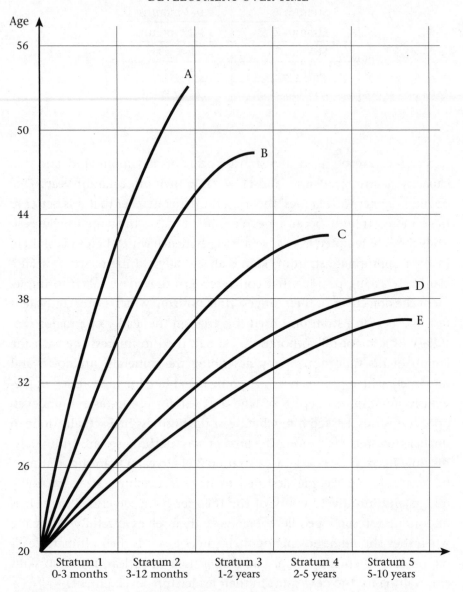

A represents a person who will reach a maximum time horizon leadership skill of stratum 2 between an age of 50 and 56
B represents a person who will reach a maximum time horizon leadership skill of stratum 3 between an age of 44 and 50
C represents a person who will reach a maximum time horizon leadership skill of stratum 4 between an age of 38 and 44
D represents a person who will reach a maximum time horizon leadership skill of stratum 5 between an age of 38 and 44
E represents a person who will reach a maximum time horizon leadership skill of stratum 5 between an age of 32 and 38

The theory predicts that each of thes leaders would demonstrate competence throughout their career, at the level predicted by their time horizon potential development line. Obviously, A will take longer to achieve a lower level of competence at a later stage in their career. Person E would be, by any standards, an astonishingly bright high-flier, who would demonstrate outstanding leadership skills from a young age throughout a glittering leadership career.

THE NATURE OF TIME HORIZONS AND THEIR IMPORTANCE IN DECISION MAKING

Given that time is a crucial factor in most decision making, from the economic and the strategic point of view, it is surprising how few academics have addressed the subject. However there are some, besides Elliott Jaques, described just above. Paul Lawrence and Jay Lorsch wrote their book, *Managing Integration and Differentiation* from their base at Harvard Business School. They analyzed the concepts of differentiation and integration, which is the phenomenon which describes how people in organizations take contradictory decisions, even though both parties to the decisions are taking them in the best interests of the business, as they see it. For example: in order to maximize revenue, the marketing manager wants the largest possible range of products and sizes to offer to customers. The production manager wants to make the smallest possible range of products in the fewest possible number of sizes, in order to minimize production costs. Both consider their preference to be in the best interests of the organization and to accord with their guidelines for their role in the business. However, as a consequence of each of these people doing their job correctly, as they see it, the organization is put in a contradictory and compromised set of positions. *Differentiation* refers to the process whereby the two managers of marketing and production respectively arrive at a differentiated, contradictory, decision. *Integration* is the process whereby the leader then has to integrate the differentiated decisions to arrive at an integrated decision in the best, overall interests of the firm.

In addition to these findings, Lawrence and Lorsch made an interesting discovery with regard to time horizons and the decision-making propensities of the managers they studied. They found that managers in different functions tended to think in different time horizons. This provides the explanatory variable which causes these managers to arrive at differentiated decisions on behalf of the business. For example, consider a research scientist and a sales manager. The former thinks in terms of time horizons of many years before hoping to see the fruits of their research. By comparison, the sales manager probably uses a time horizon of a few months when considering the decision options of the organization.

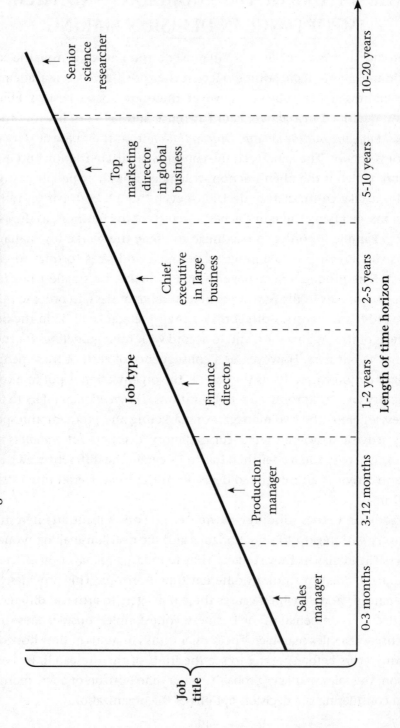

Fig. 2.2 THE EFFECTS OF ROLE UPON TIME HORIZONS

Different types of job have a particular time horizon associated with the role. This is caused by the nature of the work function and how far forward in time it is necessary to think to carry out the function properly.

Research I undertook at the London Business School, continued the work described above, of both Elliott Jaques and Lawrence and Lorsch. I wanted to find the relationship between the importance of the decisions taken by leaders and the lengths of time those decisions were intended to affect their businesses. I also enquired whether the different managers at each of the lower levels of the hierarchy of the business tended to see their part in the decision in shorter time horizons, the lower down the ladder they were. Finally, I researched whether there was a correlation between the alignment of time horizons and profitability of the business. In other words, if the time horizons are properly aligned, with the longest at the top and the shortest at the bottom, was that organization likely to be more profitable than one where the time horizons were not so well aligned?

My key findings were the following:

- Time-horizon-aligned organizations are more profitable than non-time horizon-aligned businesses.
- There is a strong correlation between the level in the hierarchy a person occupies and the length of their time horizon. Leaders nearly always have longer time horizons than the mass of people lower down the hierarchy.
- When functional managers are asked to think in integrated organizational terms, rather than in terms of their functional roles, they usually overcome the differentiating problems and the differences in their time horizons are levelled out. This implies that the policy recommendations of Lawrence and Lorsch that only top managers could integrate the differentiating problems of their more functionally controlled subordinates

> **Leaders nearly always have longer time horizons than the mass of people lower down the hierarchy.**

should be amended. The policy should be to ensure that their people learned to think in organization-wide terms rather than merely departmental, functional terms.

FIG. 2.3 TIME HORIZONS AND THEIR ASSOCIATED JOB TITLES

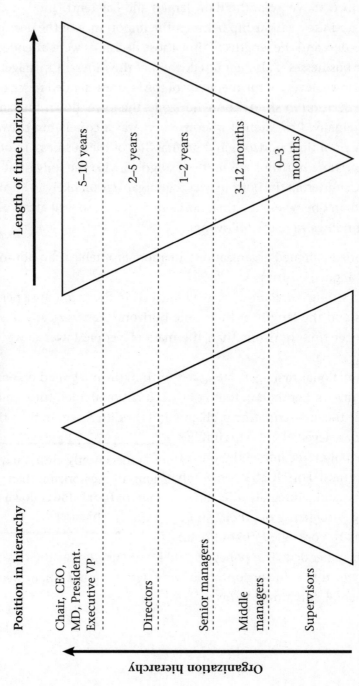

The higher up the organization, the longer the time horizon. Different jobs each have their own time horizon. The most efficient businesses have leaders with the longest time horizons, and their subordinates have ever-decreasing time horizons at each succeeding lower level in the hierarchy

All the above research findings have profound implications for every developing leader:

- leaders should try to remain continuously aware of their current and developing time horizon
- as leaders develop in their managerial roles, they should always stretch their imagination to the time horizon of their boss and see their decisions in terms of their boss's time-horizon context, rather than their own
- on occasions, when leaders realize they are seeing further in their thinking than their leader, they should understand this will appear to be threatening to their boss and they will need to exercise extreme caution. It will also indicate to them that they are ready to do their leader's job
- when they realize they are seeing further on behalf of the organization than any body else within it, they should be its leader.

The reader should reflect on his or her personal time horizon and their self-assessment for its potential growth. How far forward, in time, do you go, in your own mind, when thinking about the future of the business? Do you have a vision of what the business or industry will look like in five years time? Or are you more comfortable thinking about the one-to-two-year period? How fast is the length of your time horizon growing? What was it two years ago? How does that compare to now? How far forward do you think you will be able to cast your mind when you reach the height of your leadership powers? To get a more accurate assessment of your personal current and potential time horizon, complete Questionnaire 2.1.

Fig. 2.4 TIME-HORIZON-ALIGNED ORGANIZATIONS ARE MORE PROFITABLE THAN NON-TIME-HORIZON-ALIGNED ORGANIZATIONS

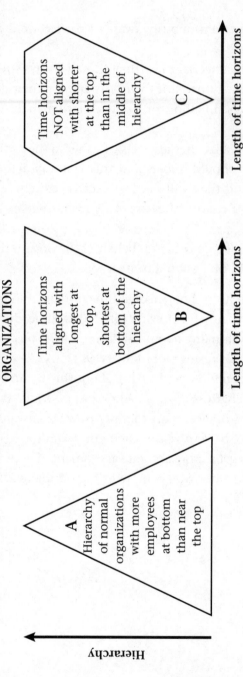

A represents a classical hierarchy with most employees at the bottom of the organization, narrowing to fewer management employees in the middle of the business, then just a few leaders at the top.

B represents a classical time-horizon alignment of a well-aligned business. Typically, this would assume that most of those at the production end of the organization need a very short time horizon to do their job. For example: a production worker needs to plan his or her work over a day or two; the supervisor will be planning a production schedule over the next month or two; the supervisor's manager will be planning a complete production cycle over the next year or two. The director of production, in charge of the production manager, may be planning a complete cycle of long-run production, renewing machinery and plant, looking for new economical sources of supply, researching new technologies to achieve a competitive edge. Finally, the CEO will be thinking in terms of a time horizon of, say, five to ten years, in order to ensure the long-term success of the business.

C represents a business where the leadership team is thinking in a shorter term than the senior executives. This leads to frustration at the lower levels, the loss of skilled personnel, excessive politicking by the leadership team and, eventually, lower profits and a less efficient organization.

Questionnaire 2.1
THE TIME-HORIZON QUESTIONNAIRE

Think about each question carefully. Try to answer honestly and accurately. Having considered each statement, tick the box which accurately describes the time period in each case.

	Up to 3 months	Up to 12 months	Up to 24 months	Up to 60 months	Up to 120 months
I can accurately and confidently predict the future of the *industry* I work in over the next					
I can accurately and confidently predict the future of the *business* I work in over the next					
I can accurately and confidently predict the future of the *division* of the business I work in over the next					
The most important decision I have taken in the past year will have an effect upon the organization over a period of					
My best subordinate will effect their part in my decision over the following time period					
My boss understands my decision will affect the organization over the following time period					
I like my boss to review my work every					
I feel comfortable when I review the work of my best subordinate every					
My best subordinate's most important decisions affect the organization over a period of					
My boss's most important decisions affect the organization over a period of					
Add the ticks in each column					
Multiply each tick by the number	3	12	24	60	120
The total for each column is					
The total added together is					
The total divided by 10 is					
Find the time horizon strata which is closest to your average	TH 1 (3)	TH 2 (12)	TH 3 (24)	TH 4 (60)	TH 5 (120)

You now have an indication of your current time horizon. It cannot be entirely accurate because some of the variables in the questions are partially an accident of current events in your business and industry. However, if you have the right leadership potential, you will always find yourself working towards where you are most comfortable in the types and importance of the decisions you have to take. As you reflect on your result consider also how old you are, how rapidly you have been developing over the past five years of your career and how many more years you are likely to work. This will indicate to you whether you are likely to move into many further strata and what level in the organization you are likely to achieve. Use Table 2.2 as a guideline.

Table 2.2 Time horizon strata and types of job in an average organization

Stratum or time horizon	Typical level in the organization
1 (0–3 months)	Foreperson or supervisor
2 (3–12 months)	Junior to middle management
3 (1-2 years)	Middle to senior management
4 (2–5 years)	Senior management to director
5 (5–10 years)	Managing director, chairperson, executive VP or president

Of course, different industries use various job titles and some of the titles in the table may not be relevant to the reader's industry. Further, one should take into account that the leader in a business with revenue of £300m and 1000 employees probably requires a much shorter time horizon than the same title leading an organization with a revenue of £10bn and 100 000 staff. Yet both may carry the same leader's title of *managing director*. Management science has not yet developed enough classification systems and definitions to achieve the necessary precision. Some leaders pay attention to job titles because so many other decision makers care unduly about such matters. I have known people

The right choice of the type of industry or business you work in will make a considerable difference to your chances of success.

leave their organization, when offered promotion, because the larger and more interesting task on offer did not carry the title 'Director' and they felt they would be losing an important factor in their career development.

Managing a leadership career over a long period is complex and difficult. There will be mishaps and periods of faster and slower growth. The right choice of the type of industry or business you work in will make a considerable difference to your chances of success.

WHAT TYPES OF COMPANY SHOULD YOU WORK FOR?

By definition, most industries contain some good leaders. They tend to distribute themselves randomly. The criteria of choice at the beginning of a career should always be, 'what is it that interests me?' It is wise to choose subjects and industries which attract you and arouse your curiosity. It will be during the early part of your career that you get involved in the nitty-gritty aspects of business. You will be close to the rock face and will need some genuine interest to keep you going.

However, if your preferences give you some latitude, try to choose an industry which is at a relatively early point in its development cycle, or about to undergo a long-term fresh impetus in its development. If you do have a choice, select a business which is considered to be either the best performer in the industry, or the organization with a leading market share, or with some technological innovation which ensures its competitive edge. If appropriate, it should be international. Most modern leadership careers will involve some spell abroad. Above all, you should be *excited* about the products of your business and industry and about working for it (but without losing your dispassion).

The type of business, and its stage of evolution, will become less important as your career advances. The challenges, later in your career, will be about achieving strategic vision and ensuring that you make a success of leading whatever workforce you have at your disposal. You will learn to choose your leadership style according to the culture of the business and the state of the organization. Your choices will be made from a wide and varied repertoire because great leaders are not constrained by the smaller range of choices that lesser managers, without your power and self-control, have to choose from.

Type of industry

As each generation starts its career, (which is, of course, a continuous process), people have to ask themselves 'what industry or business will enable me to maximize my enjoyment of my working life and optimize the return on my talents'. In earlier days it was probably easier, because technology and industrial cycles evolved more slowly. Thus, someone entering the 19th-century rail industry could be reasonably confident that they would have a lifetime's career within the industry or even the same organization. The same may have applied to the airline travel industry in the 20th century. But who can predict how long some of the industrial sectors of the late-20th century will endure? Consider, for example, the food distribution industry in the UK. At the time of writing (1998) it is dominated by three gigantic retail businesses (Sainsbury, Tesco and Asda) which specialize in super- or hypermarkets, and which attract large populations of consumers to travel to them. But as the power and ubiquity of the Internet system expands, that pattern of behaviour for most of their customers will seem, increasingly, a waste of time. Most of their purchases are repetitions of brand purchases, which do not vary from week to week. Travel to and from the supermarket is time-consuming and the endless waste of energy involved in putting products in and out of wire baskets is, frankly, a form of ritual, collective madness. When Internet systems are available widely enough, most people may well order the majority of their repeat purchases for home delivery, from their own Internet web site. The whole industry of food distribution will be revolutionized, although we cannot foretell exactly how. Anybody who enters that industry cannot possible foresee what kind of work they will be doing in ten years' time. That has two implications. The first is that people starting careers at the turn of the millennium should be prepared to change their career path, industry sector and type of skills and work several times throughout their career. Second, those who desire stability should be looking to the great emerging industries which will dominate the 21st century, if they wish to maximize the stability of their career. The great industries of the 21st century will be almost certainly be among those listed in Table 2.3.

Table 2.3 The great growth industries of the 21st century

Industry sector	Reason for its dominance
Food supply and logistics	Because the problem of the 21st century will be about food distribution, rather than food production.
Communication channels	Because communications along fibre rather than copper channels will be the key to the intimate interconnection with the distribution problem of the 21st century, as well as the means of educating and communicating on the www. Also, because it may be that control of the channels will give opportunities for massive profits (although it is likely that governments will regulate the capacity to extract these profits, with taxes on entertainment equivalent to the 20th-century taxes on petroleum and alcohol).
Entertainment distribution	Because the dissemination of hegemonic culture will be the key to domination in the 21st century and will, hopefully, replace the warfare that dominated the 20th century.
Travel	Because as the need to travel for communication purposes decreases, the desirability of travel and tourism, for pleasure, will increase.
Leisure	Because the leisure industries are taking an increasing percentage of the spare time and income of both employed and unemployed.

There are still valid reasons for finding a stable path for a career. The first is that, if you choose an industry which really interests you, then it is more fun to pursue it than being forced to turn to your second or third choice, later on in your career, if you have to change jobs. Second, a stable career in any one industry will lead to continuously increasing knowledge and thus a greater degree of knowledge. This, in turn, will give you a greater return on the economic 'rent' of your knowledge, as more people will know about you and be prepared to pay for your accumulation of experience. Third, your real usefulness will be enhanced by stability; the effect of maximizing your personal economic rents will also mean a greater level of income. Finally, it is advisable to stay with the new industries because, by and large, they will be where the higher profits will be made over the longest period.

What condition should your ideal employing firm be in?

Try to choose relatively healthy businesses in the early stages of your career. These businesses will not be living off past glories. They should have excellent development programmes for young employees, especially management trainees (if that is your preferred entry point). The business you choose should be one of the top three controllers of market share, because they are usually the largest profit earners in any industry. Enquire whether it has a reputation for being over-staffed and whether it is ruthless about discarding people; this will indicate whether it has a decent humanitarian approach. Remember that many leaders do not necessarily shine in their first few years, and you do not want a dismissal to show as a black mark in your résumé, so choose an organization with a reputation for dealing fairly with people. A further consideration should be that in a better quality business there is a probability that a potential great leader may be treated better and with more understanding than in a second-rate, 'hire and fire' organization where the management may not be capable of realizing how good a potential leader is, and dismiss him/her for being wayward (a customary mannerism in younger potential leaders). There will also be more opportunities in one of the larger, more successful companies that a senior manager will recognize you for the good leader you could become. In a more benign organization you are less likely to attract jealousy from lesser managers who might try to forestall your career. One meets many excessively 'political' people in the early stages of a career who may just do damage for damage's sake! Quality organizations get rid of such individuals, if they get in at all. Finally, almost all the Peter Principle people (those who have been promoted to a job at their level of incompetence) will be clustered at the lower levels of management.

How to choose which business or industries to join

If you intend to move around in your career, from one business to another, there are different considerations to take into account at each stage. The organization you join should depend on which particular stage of your career you have achieved.

Table 2.4 Choice of selection criteria at different stages of a leadership career

Beginning	Mid-career	Final stages/peak of leadership skills
Choose firms which have a 'Rolls-Royce' reputation.	You should change only for firms that offer an accelerated route to the top.	Try to choose firms with great brands which are run down, rather than great companies which are nearing exhaustion.
Choose firms which have the number one, two or three position in terms of market share.	You can risk a poor reputation company – but you should investigate that it is not fallibly flawed.	The test question should be 'are you prepared to spend the rest of your career there?'
Get a job which offers management training. It will save you the time it takes to get an MBA-type qualification.	Only move to businesses whose size can match your business abilities. Not worth being a big fish in a small pond, nor a small fish in a big pond. Get a pond which matches your size!	Don't move to a position where ultimate power resides with the idiot who screwed up the company before they started looking for you, unless you can see how to remove the problem.
		Scrutinise the non-executive officers and directors and judge whether you can achieve a working relationship with them – and they won't panic while allowing you a rational amount of time for you to achieve the leadership job.

At every stage of your career you should be asking yourself four key questions. They are :

1 What particular skills you are developing?
2 Are you undergoing trauma without being aware?
3 What is your instinctive feel for your colleagues'/subordinates' work skills?
4 What kind of people and skills are *not* represented in your team, thus leading you to ask what types you should try to recruit?

Try the following diagnostic guide in Questionnaire 2.2 to test how well you are using these criteria. Every time your career coincides with a lateral line, and has done so in the past, consider your career management to be on track. Every time that it doesn't or isn't, ask yourself to justify why not.

Questionnaire 2.2
MATCHING CAREER STAGE, BUSINESS CONDITION AND LEADERSHIP STYLE

Stage of career	Condition of the business	Your leadership style	Allocate points
Pre-management jobs	mature, wealthy people developer; mentoring system in place	team work highly honed; gaining recognition; egalitarian	6 for three in alignment 4 for two in alignment
First management role	Relatively mature businesses in highly competitive industries; profits low but revenue increasing rapdily	determined forceful learning democratic partnership approach	10 for three in alignment 8 for two in alignment
Middle management	high profits; products moving into more mature phases; many opportunities to prove skills	authoritative confident highly visible firmly sighted on the next promotion	14 for three in alignment 10 for two in alignment
Senior management	low to medium profits; using brands to maintain position in industry; trying to consolidate gains of the past	solid no mistakes careful gaining trust creating feelings of invincibility reliable	20 for three in alignment 14 for two in alignment
First directorship	personal contract of minimum 12 months notice; business solid enough to be able to meet obligations	sensitive knowledgeable strategic loyal overtly ethical	24 for three in alignment 16 for two in alignment
First MDship	business should be in condition to suit your own knowledge of skills and style	visionary inspirational decent great user of time	28 for three in alignment 20 for two in alignment
TOTAL	*Add the scores you have circled* < 40: your leadership career is in trouble–focus more 41–80: average potential; time to try harder still 81–100: your leadership career is well launched		

HOW DO LEADERS AVOID CAREER ACCIDENTS?

Leaders should always try to be circumspect. At any time in their career, whatever they do, they owe a duty to themselves and others to try to foresee, how others will perceive their action. I constantly find leaders being surprised at their managers' and staffs' reactions to, or interpretations of, their behaviour and/or actions. For example, I remember one leader who gained a reputation for sexual abuse of the secretaries at his head office. I tackled him on this subject, at the request of the non-executive directors of the company, who were worried about (1) his possible lack of concentration on the company's performance and (2) the possibility of the company attracting adverse publicity if his behaviour got into the media. When I asked him about it I found that he had, in fact, been separated from his wife for over two years. He had been living with one of the company's senior managers, who was employed in one of the corporation's regional offices. It was a permanent relationship and he had not indulged in any improper conduct. I had to explain to him that, as leader, it wasn't only his actual conduct which counted, but how it was seen by his employees. Since, ultimately, some employees will always indulge in speculation and circulate rumours it is vital that leaders be circumspect and never feed ammunition to the rumour mill. Leaders too easily forget that they are *always* a centre of attention and that whatever they do will be carefully scrutinized. This is an aspect of the 'goldfish bowl' in which leaders live their lives which can sometimes feel a little onerous. However, compared to the fun and rewards of leadership, a little circumspection gets it all into perspective. It is just part of the job description of leadership.

HOW DO YOU DEAL WITH SETBACKS?

Everybody suffers setbacks in their career, sometimes as a consequence of the actions of other people; at other times from one's own lack of ability. Occasionally, it's just the nature of natural events going against you for a while. So always be ready to return to the drawing board, whether for strategic insight or to understand the latest economic and social circumstances of your decision making. One of the cleverest men I ever knew became a leading professor at Oxford. He always retained the habit of attending student lectures whenever a new topic or research area emerged that he felt he ought to understand. Sitting at the back of the lecture hall, with the rest of the students, did him a lot of good, as he ingested fresh knowledge. It also had an amazing effect upon his staff and other lecturers. If the great man himself could return to the drawing board to learn new things, they were all motivated both to keep their humility carefully wrapped around their tendency to self-importance and to keep their knowledge up to date.

> **Occasionally, it's just the nature of natural events going against you for a while. So always be ready to return to the drawing board.**

Another accident-avoidance procedure is to never take on the bigger jobs in your career until you are ready. Early exposure to jobs and responsibilities you are not prepared for, and cannot yet master, will always carry the danger of breaking your spirit and moral fibre. With that gone, you will be utterly lost.

You must understand that leadership skills are, usually, general skills and they can be exploited in many industries – more so as you get older and wiser. This means that, if yours is a career that is going to be constructed from several different jobs in various businesses, you will need to find the courage to try different industries. It is great fun and may prove to you that your leadership skills are a multi-purpose set of tools that can be applied to many situations and industrial sectors. It may also offer a more stimulating career.

Here I should state, for the record, that I hold several personal guidelines which seem relevant to business. First, most of the wise people I see at work in leadership roles, rarely, if ever, over-indulge in alcohol and they never take drugs. If you can control it, it is wise to never lose your temper. If you need to *appear angry*, do so under strictly controlled circumstances. Appearing to lose your temper may be useful on rare occasions, to influence the behaviour you want from your people, or to emphasize the importance of some action by them or their subordinates. Genuine temper is rarely a useful tool. Even when it seems to be appropriate, it is a blunt rather than a sharp instrument of leadership effectiveness. Why? Because it is hard to predict individual's personal response to anger and, therefore, the learning they will take away from any temper you display with the intention of getting them to behave in a particular way.

Another of my dicta is that wise leaders don't join companies where the installed leader looks like a *nominal leader* (as defined above). He will only wish to use your skills and will give you neither credit nor satisfaction. Similarly, do not work for insecure bosses – they are the most dangerous beings on earth. The better you are, the more they will fear you. Their fear will make them behave irrationally, jealously and nastily. Few people can cope well with the easy and natural brilliance of rivals and subordinates. If you cannot see a surefire way of removing a nominal or inferior leader at an early date, when offered a job, don't take it!

> **Wise leaders don't join companies where the installed leader looks like a *nominal leader*.**

LAST WORDS

This chapter has demonstrated that leadership is a career choice available to those who have 'the leadership gene'. Every leader has an optimum time horizon he will have developed to when their career matures. With that in mind, I advise prospective leaders to manage their careers from the beginning, by carefully nurturing their skills, developing a high quality personal life and living always by carefully considered ethically based values.

RECOMMENDED READING FOR CHAPTER 2

Belbin, R M. (1991) *Management Teams*. Oxford: Butterworth Heinemann.

Belbin, M. (1993) *Team Roles at Work*. Oxford: Butterworth Heinemann.

Chapman, E. N. (1977) *Your Attitude is Showing*. Palo Alto, CA: Science Research Associates Inc.

Covey, S. R. (1989) *The 7 Habits of Highly Effective People*. New York: Simon & Schuster.

Cox, D. L. (1993) *Management Fleas & Leadership Flies*. Burton-on-Trent and Derby: Tresises.

Ferrucci, P. (1990) *What We May Be*. London: Aquarian/Thorsons.

Harris, T. A. (1973) *I'm OK – You're OK*. London: Pan.

Herder, J. (1992) *The Tao of Leadership*. Aldershot: Gower.

Jaques, E. (1976) *A General Theory of Bureaucracy*. London: Heinemann.

Jaques, E. (1982a) *The Form of Time*. London: Heinemann.

Jaques, E. (1982b) *Free Enterprise, Fair Employment*. London: Heinemann.

Kakabadse, A. (1991) *The Wealth Creators*. London: Kogan Page.

Kepner, C. H. and Tregoe, B. B. (1965) *The Rational Manager*. New York: McGraw-Hill.

Lawrence, P. R. and Lorsch, J. W. (1967) *Managing Integration and Differentiation*. Cambridge, MA: Harvard University Press.

Levicki, C. J. (1983) *Managerial time horizons and decision making and their effects on organisational performance*. unpub. PhD thesis, London: London University Business School.

Levicki, C. J. (1996) *The Strategy Workout*. London: Financial Times Pitman Publishing.

Lewis, R. and Lowe, P. (1992) *Individual Excellence*. London: Kogan Page.

McClelland, D. (1961) *The Achieving Society*. Princeton, NJ: Van Nostrand.

Peter, L. J. and Hull, R. (1979) *The Peter Principle*. London: Pan.

White, R. P., Hodgson, P. and Crainer, S. (1996) *The Future of Leadership*. London: Financial Times Pitman Publishing.

Biographies of companies and leaders

Bramson, A. (1990) *Pure Luck*. Wellingborough: Patrick Stephens.

Burrough, D. and Jelyar, J. (1990) *Barbarians at the Gate*. London: Jonathan Cape.

Colier, P. and Horowitz, D. (1976) *The Rockefellers*. New York: Signet.

Davies, H. (1981) *The Grades*. London: Weidenfeld & Nicolson.

Gittin, N. and Masters, K. (1997) *Hit and Run*. New York: Simon & Schuster.

Heller, R. (1993) *The Super Chiefs*. New York: Truman Talley/Plume.

Lenzner, R. (1985) *The Great Getty*. New York: Signet.

Love, J. F. (1995) *McDonald's: Behind the Arches*. New York: Bantam.

Maney, K. (1995) *Megamedia Shakeout*. New York: John Wiley.

Morita, A. (1994) *Made in Japan*. London: HarperCollins.

Shawcross, W. (1992) *Murdoch*. London: Chatto & Windus.

Sloan, A. P. (1965) *My Years with General Motors*. New York: MacFadden-Bartell.

Thompson, P. (1990) *Sharing the Success*. London: Fontana.

Walton, S. (1993) *Made in America*. New York: Bantam.

LEADERSHIP AND LIFE

....

This chapter will discuss the balance between
having a leadership career and managing a full
private life. It emphasizes that achieving a
fulfilled overall life requires a balance between
time allocated to business and the personal
roles (although every individual's equilibrium
will be different). And most leaders need a
good 'partner' – choose carefully!

....

EMOTIONAL INTELLIGENCE AND MATURITY

Great leadership requires emotional intelligence. I will explain more about the meaning of this phrase below. Emotional maturity helps you to have a rewarding private life. To further develop my thesis of the real difference between strategic leaders and nominal leaders, let me make clear another difference between these two species of leader. Nominal leaders have a *need to lead*; effective leaders have a *need to achieve* (*see* McClelland 1961). The need to lead of nominal leaders often arises from a lack of emotional balance caused by behaviours such as parental manipulation of the child's desire to please ('You only got 99 out of a 100 in your math's test? Where did you lose the other mark?'). The need to achieve of strategic leaders is anchored in a childhood upbringing based upon emotional balance, thus enabling the child to acquire a full range of emotions. This, in turn, enables them to match their talent and their expectations of themselves and others.

The leaders I am describing tend to realize, at a fairly young age, that they have prospects of having a full life. They probably don't interpret this to mean that they are likely to finish their career at the top of an organization. More likely, they will realize that with reasonable luck and self-control they will have a materially secure and emotionally contented life and will choose the paths in their career and personal life accordingly. Quite early in their career they will have realized that they are above average in potential and skills. If their range of skills and qualities is lacking anything in particular they will know whether it is remediable. If they need further training they will realise this. If their emotional intelligence and maturity is not as well developed as their strategic thinking power, it will have to be strengthened in order to make themselves truly fit for leadership. Above all they know they will need a thorough balance to make really correct strategic judgements.

What is emotional intelligence?

In his book, *Emotional Intelligence*, Daniel Goleman (1996) describes the bases of interpersonal intelligence as consisting of four components:

1 organizing groups (the skill of initiating and co-ordinating the efforts of others)
2 negotiating solutions (the talent of preventing conflicts or resolving those that flare up)
3 personal connection (the talent of empathizing and connecting)
4 social analysis (the ability to detect and have insights about people's feelings, motives and concerns)

He goes on to explain:

> Taken together, these skills are the stuff of interpersonal polish, the necessary ingredients for charm, social success, even charisma ... They [people with these skills] are the natural leaders, the people who can express the unspoken collective sentiment and articulate it so as to guide a group towards its goals ... [they] evoke the comment, 'What a pleasure to be around someone like that.'

The roots of emotional intelligence come from a capacity to empathize with others and to feel what they feel. It also comes from controlling one's moods and ensuring that passing feelings do not control one's behaviour. People with emotional intelligence take their decisions about themselves and others based on balanced views about what they really think and feel, not on temporary, passing moods. How do mature people know it is a genuine insight rather than a mood based upon a passing feeling? Goleman explains that moods are caused by automated, non-controlled and, sometimes, irrational reactions to previous events in your life. These may have been occasions of deep sadness, cruelty or nastiness by some people around you or just an accident which left a traumatic scar upon your psyche. These psychological scars from the past can cause you to react and behave in an automated manner to a particular current event which sets off those switches in your mind based on the traumatic event from the past. Even though you may realize that this is happening to you, until you learn to control yourself fully, you will remain unable to do anything about it, other than go with the force of the passing mood. You will know that you are reacting in a way the current event does not merit,

> People with emotional intelligence take their decisions about themselves and others based on balanced views about what they really think and feel, not on temporary, passing moods.

whether reacting too weakly or too strongly. But you will feel powerless until you know how to control the mood, rather than have it control you.

Furthermore, such events may cause you stress or otherwise create feelings which cause you to react inappropriately to other events or circumstances. For example, you have a bad day at the office. That evening you go home and shout at your partner. The latter has nothing to do with the causes of your bad feeling. Your partner's role is not to serve as a catharsis for your bad day at the office. It was thus an entirely inappropriate reaction and may also make you feel even worse because you are probably aware that your behaviour is counter-productive. Now you will have a bad evening at home, as well as a bad day at the office!

Getting control of yourself, and behaving sensibly under all circumstances, can be defined as emotional intelligence and maturity. This does not mean not knowing how to enjoy yourself. It means you do your merrymaking under safe circumstances and when the enjoyment is pure and will have no adverse consequences for yourself or others. I am not advocating an excess of control, or being cold-blooded. I am merely saying that quality people, those who are destined to be or become great leaders know how to manage a balanced life. This will include *all* the pleasures life offers, whether they are based on physical or mental pleasure or the profoundly conceptual or utterly superficial. Once again, we are talking about a balanced life.

Most people dismiss the possibility that they could control themselves better. They feel it is too difficult when, and if, they acknowledge there is any problem in that area. They tell themselves that, even though they are intelligent and can recognize that their behaviour is either unreasonable or stupid, they cannot control their moods in the disciplined way being advocated. Let's face it, it is very hard to control *everything*. Those who wish to become, and make themselves fit to be, great and effective leaders, steel themselves to do it and succeed, in the main. These people realize that those irrational reactions to the wrong stimuli are almost always based upon behaviours and reactions learned, subconsciously, during childhood. The lessons were wrongly learned and can be unlearned. Strategic leaders do something about it. They retrain themselves to be fit for their purposes: leadership.

Case study 3.1

ALASTAIR IN SEARCH OF HIS LEADERSHIP SOUL

Alastair is a client whose job is to lead the entertainment division of a large overseas retail business. My ostensible objective was to help him revise the strategic vision of his business, a division of a group on whose board he sat. However, when analyzing the psychometrics of Alastair's team, his personal results caused me deep concern. They indicated a man who had high levels of anger and who also appeared to be profoundly unhappy. I asked him if he had suffered from any physical sickness which could be associated with stress. He had been treated for high blood pressure the previous year. These physical signs confirmed the psychometric results were accurate.

Upon investigation I discovered the underlying cause of his stress was his (subconscious) feeling that he had to spend his life replacing the father who disappeared from his life when he was six. As a consequence he never relaxed at work. He had little sense of humour and could not understand subordinates who did not do their duty constantly.

He had never felt he had a right to happiness in his personal life. Although he had married he had never experienced joy. Fortunately he had married a charming and very relaxed woman. However, for 27 years he had verbally abused her, usually as a consequence of things not going well for him at the office.

After I told him my analysis of his psychometric results, he admitted that he was a deeply unhappy man. He confessed that his wife had told him she could not take any more. Because she still loved him, in spite of all the unhappiness he had caused her. She was simply unable to absorb any more temper tantrums or Alastair's inability to relax and be happy.

Solution and its consequences

I met with Alastair and his wife and facilitated a new social compact between them.

Alastair has now begun to learn to relax and have more fun in his private life. He now apologizes to his wife when he shouts at her and shouts a lot less than he used to. He is practicing the idea of relaxation and taking life a little less seriously. He has become a major user of 'helicopter theory' (Chapter 5) and is being appreciated much more by his fellow directors on the group board.

CAN YOU HELP YOURSELF?

How can you know if any imbalances, incorrect instincts or inappropriate automatic responses exist in your own range of behaviours? First, study the way people react to you. Second, you can tell because, by and large, we do know when we are behaving irrationally. We all tend to tolerate ourselves too easily and delude ourselves that we cannot do anything about it. Force yourself to ask what you can do to repair and rebuild any imbalances, incorrect instincts or irrational responses, in your own profile? There are always solutions. What are they?

First, read as much as possible of the literature on emotional intelligence and balance as you can (see the recommended reading at the end of this chapter). Investigate your childhood deeply and carefully, first, from your own memories, then from family members (siblings can be particularly useful). Ask those who observed your upbringing. Although they can never give you completely neutral views on your childhood nor your parents' strengths and weaknesses, they can be informative. You can question close childhood friends, friends' parents, neighbours and others relations of the family. Try to achieve a sense of neutrality about their various observations of events. Then work hard to make fresh interpretations of any events and actions from your past that may have caused any current irrational, automated responses in your behaviour patterns. Most of us have some. Remember, also, that it is unlikely that they were caused by any intentional ill will on the part of parents or guardians.

> If you are really unable to get new perspectives and change behaviours which you know are irrational and deleterious to your life, you may need to consider going to a professional therapist.

They may just be the result of your own accidental and incorrect interpretation of events by yourself (for which you will, of course, forgive yourself when you sort it out).

If you are really unable to get new perspectives and change behaviours which you know are irrational and deleterious to your life, you may need to consider going to a professional therapist. Ensure it is somebody who really understands the nature of business life and its tremendous pressures on leaders.

Getting your emotional life sorted out must be at least as important as your business life. After all, you owe it to yourself to try to be happy. It is the right thing to do and it has no potential adverse indicators. I have met some leaders who were particularly unhappy. They thought they would never know happiness and had grown accustomed to thinking that they, somehow, had missed the 'happiness gene'. They were enormously buoyed up by my insistence that everybody has a right to be happy and that they owed it to themselves to find out what was preventing them from enjoying their lives. In several cases these people managed to change their lives and, as I would put it, start living a full life of satisfaction at work and contentment at home.

THE CONNECTIONS BETWEEN CORRECT BEHAVIOUR AND ETHICS

The beginning of an answer to large questions such as 'what's the point of living?' is to acknowledge that we really do have choices to be happy or sad. Neither is a given. This knowledge is the great consequential benefit of the breakthrough in understanding human psychology, following the seminal work of Freud, Jung and the other founder theorists of different schools of psychological analysis. They have proved that how we feel is a consequence of either inherited characteristics, genetic traits, chemical imbalances in our bodies or behaviours learned unconsciously and subconsciously during the impressionable years when growing up. Although we cannot control all these given or 'learned responses' when we acquire them in our childhood, (no matter how they get attributed to us), we can control their effects upon us by relearning and modifying our behaviour when we are adults. We merely have to be determined to avoid unnecessary suffering, when we realize that that is what we are suffering from or inflicting upon others.

In the late 20th century, most intelligent people realize they have a right to be happy and that the means exist for them to achieve this, in spite of the fact that they may have some learned responses which make them feel they don't automatically have that right. We all have both the opportunity and the choice to be happy. Being happy also implies that you can be good to yourself and do good to others. First, however, you have to be sure you know when you are happy. Many business people I work with like to believe they are happy when busy at work but, often, they don't look happy to me. Usually, when questioned, they agree they are not happy, but are too busy to think about their happiness. Indeed, they often don't know how to think about such matters at all. Once they learn how to open the debate in their own minds, they realize that what they have been calling 'happiness' is actually only frenetic activity ('busyness') dressed up by themselves to substitute for happiness.

Assuming that you can help yourself achieve some relief from unhappiness, the next key question is 'can you be happy in yourself while behaving badly towards others?' Self-evidently, if you treat yourself badly, you cannot be or make yourself happy. Another consequence of this argument would lead you to conclude that if you treat others badly you are reducing their happiness. This is not only an unethical position, but it cannot be in the interests of your business either, which further implies that you ought to try to be good to others, (including employees), as well as to yourself.

If we can agree with the logical line so far, that being good is a choice and a wise one at that, one must also agree that to have a choice to do good and choose *not* to exercise it, would be close to what those who believe in it, would call a mortal sin. This assumes, of course, that all behaviour has a moral content, in that good behaviour is also ethically desirable behaviour. This makes being and doing good not only a desirable choice but also a moral imperative.

What are ethics and why are they relevant?

Ethics refer to the underlying principles of life which can, could or should govern the way we behave, live and react to others. Can the same principles govern both our business and our private lives? If not, why not? Following this rationale, given that we spend similar amounts of our conscious time at both work and play, it is surely irrational to choose to be happy and moral in one part of our lives and not in the other.

> It must surely make sense to behave well and take good decisions that have good consequences, both in one's personal life and in any organizational decisions one has to make as a leader.

All behaviour has moral implications. Further, if good behaviour and good actions are ethically desirable and bad actions and bad behaviour are ethically undesirable, we have also demonstrated that whatever behaviour we choose to adopt we are also consciously adopting its underlying value (even if we choose to ignore or remain unaware that there is a value implied). All this applies equally to business life as to private life. It must surely make sense to behave well and take good decisions that have good consequences, both in one's personal life and in any organizational decisions one has to make as a leader.

Examine the classical leader's dilemma of reducing the size of a business to better balance the human resources with the other resources of the business (both physical and technological). This may be necessary, because if one doesn't decrease the number of jobs, one may end by losing the whole business and all the jobs are lost. During the 'downsizing' (what a ghastly word!) exercise, you come across an employee who is marginal in terms of employability, but who is the only breadwinner for a family where the spouse is dying of cancer and one of the two children is physically and mentally handicapped. Is there an ethical or moral issue?

> Life cannot be subdivided into different realms of ethics. There cannot be two standards. There must be some universal laws which should regulate all human interaction.

In my opinion, there can be no ethics-free choice of behaviour. If we make the employee redundant, ignoring the moral imperatives, we are committing an immoral act. That must have consequences for the individual, for ourselves and for the organization. For example if we ignore our own sense of decency and fairness, the other employees who are kept on will know that management takes decisions which are callous and inhumane. This will reduce their feelings of loyalty and the manner in which they work with customers. I have experienced some cases when the employing organization has behaved so cruelly that the employees retaliated by physically sabotaging the organization's technology (IT and buildings), causing tremendous damage to the business's resources and its reputation with customers.

Would you want to treat this employee (with the family problems) any differently than you would a friend or acquaintance in your private life? Surely the same rationale must apply to business employees and colleagues as it would to personal friends. Life cannot be subdivided into different realms of ethics. There cannot be two standards. There must be some universal laws which should regulate all human interaction. Once you adopt only relative values which are, like clothes, put on and taken off according to whim or weather, what criteria can you use to differentiate the values you use at work from those which govern your domestic behaviour? How will you decide where the limits of decency are? You cannot, because there are no criteria with which to differentiate. If you adopt a lower or different standard at work from your home values, which will be the 'real' you? Will you be proud of yourself as a parent or partner in marriage, but ashamed of yourself as a leader?

I would go so far as to advocate that there should always be a mental 'ethics' file in every leader's head that is used to filter or 'litmus test' every decision and action he or she takes, to ensure that all potential breaches of decency will be avoided and that the circumstances of each and every individual in the organization are kept in mind at all times.

To summarize: there can be no values-free behaviour. If the objective of living is to have a rounded and happy (= good) life, nobody will want to employ different and potentially contradictory values in others parts of his or her life. This would result in the nonsense of living morally for some aspects of life and immorally for others. Consequently it is incumbent upon everybody to think through what their values and ethics really are and then live their lives by them. This is even more relevant if you are a leader, because your decisions and behaviours, by definition, affect many other people's lives as well as your own.

Some further random thoughts, to win over the doubters

If your behaviour at home reflects your best values, why would you want to take second-rate ethics to work with you? Don't you need them even more at work where the objectives are, after all, mainly, just to make more money? And if you're a leader, what are you doing to your employees with these 'second rate ethics'?

If your ethics at work are your *better* ethics, what kind of self-respect can you have if you value your personal life less than your business life? Remember the old adage: nobody said on their deathbed, 'I wish I'd spent more time at the office, and I'm pleased I was good there rather than at home!' Remember also that as a leader, if your life is unbalanced, you may find it impossible to take rational decisions on behalf of your employees who must be one of your most important resources.

You never know when something could go wrong. Would you want your wife or husband in a divorce court of law telling the world about the worst aspects of your personality? This is an interesting test of most people's behaviour. Consider the case study of Alastair, above. How embarrassed would you be in a court of law with your employees telling the world what kind of awful person you can be (whether you are at work or home).

A good life in the round, both at work and domestically, is the simplest. All double standards are a form of duplicity. Remember, you will be your own victim. Why do it to yourself? Ultimately, double or contradictory standards are dangerous to the leader's mental health and invidious for the welfare of the organization. They are generally bad practice. Which brings us to the question, 'When did you last examine your ethics?'

Try Questionnaire 3.1 on page 82.

Further thoughts on the relationship between ethics and behaviour

Think about some of the questions in Questionnaire 3.1. Question 4 examines the time you spend with your family. If you work long hours and expect others to do so as well, how carefully can you consider those who have more pressing family responsibilities than you. After all, some might be great potential leaders who may have chosen to sacrifice their leadership career for a sick partner or parent. What is the right thing to do? Consider further question 16 in the questionnaire. If you sometimes tell lies, when will you know that you have reached a point where it is a big lie rather than a white lie? Really wise and great leaders are skilled enough in mind and situation to ensure they never need to resort to telling any form of lie.

Questionnaire 3.1
A QUESTION OF VALUES

	Question	Yes	No	Varies	Score
1	I believe there are limits to how much time anybody should spend at work	1	3	2	
2	I shout at home but never at work	3	0	1	
3	When I have to choose, I'd take an economic decision rather than a compassionate decision	3	0	1	
4	I care about my family	3	1	2	
5	I regularly work more that 60 hours a week	3	1	2	
6	I mainly see my family at weekends	3	1	2	
7	I try not to mix personal and business socializing	0	3	2	
8	I see (saw) little of my children during weekdays	3	0	2	
9	I am religious but I would not share that information with colleagues at work	2	0	1	
10	I am sometimes distracted by the opposite sex at work	3	0	2	
11	I suspend all rules for the company Christmas party	3	0	2	
12	My salary depends on what the market will bear regardless of what the company can afford	3	1	2	
13	You cannot keep expenses records to the nearest penny/cent, it's impossible	3	0	2	
14	You have to discard people development if the firm is really sick	2	0	1	
15	I see no limit to the level of job I could achieve	3	0	2	
16	You have to tell lies at work and home	3	0	2	
17	Rules do not apply to leaders – they create rules	3	0	2	
Total					

Interpretation

Scores over 36 suggest you must carefully and immediately rethink your value system.

Scores below 20 suggest that you have thought through your ethics and behaviours.

Scores between 20 and 35 suggest that you should rethink your ethics and behaviours carefully and try to adjust them for their effects upon those you lead.

CLEVERNESS AND WISDOM

I make a strong distinction between clever people and wise people. It is becoming an accepted wisdom that great leaders need high quality emotional maturity and empathy and that this is more important than intellectual calculating power. This highlights the distinction I make between cleverness and wisdom. Clever people are the classical high achievers at university, they gain high honours and come top of the class; wise people have emotional maturity and leave college with a profound understanding of human nature; they know what they wish to achieve in life and how they intend to do it. Cleverness is based on the mental accumulation of facts and the power to juggle them; wisdom is based upon the insight of knowing what to do about the facts for everybody's good. Cleverness is the cold, calculating logic of syllogisms and specious objectivity, maximizing shareholders' wealth alone; wisdom is the ability to take optimal decisions on the grounds of both business and humanity, looking after both people and everybody's wealth.

> Cleverness is based on the mental accumulation of facts and the power to juggle them; wisdom is based upon the insight of knowing what to do about the facts for everybody's good.

What kind of partner should a leader choose (and what's wrong with love)?

I am going to make an outrageous claim here, but my experience proves it to be true and useful. I am suggesting that there is such a thing as an *appropriate partner* for a leader. Some readers will consider that choosing a partner for life as a background scenario to a leadership career is close to blasphemy. However, let me clarify the point that is being made. I am not suggesting that business leaders should go out looking to acquire a suitable business partner, rather than a partner for life. Rather, I am suggesting that simply waiting to fall in love with whoever turns up may be invidious. In reality, what really happens is that wise people don't simply select a partner on the basis of their career nor on the basis of the type of the private life they wish to lead (although both will apply to some extent). What really happens is that they tend to be selective when they fall in love. It isn't that they do not let their heart lead them; they just control their heart better and only allow their feelings to lead them to where the possible outcomes are complementary to their objectives. In other words, they do fall in love – but only with the right person! They know it is the right person because they understand themselves and they will know when they have met somebody who will know how to cope with their career, even if this person has a career of their own to pursue. The right partner will respect the inner drive and energy of the person they are attached to; they will care as much about your happiness as their own. In short, they will be faithful to what you need them to be, when they need to be a successful partner to the leader. In many modern couples, where both partners may have equally demanding careers, the ideal partner will be adaptable enough to fulfil the role of the company spouse when that role is required by their partner. With luck, and wise choice, both partners will have similarly strong ethical values. Above all, both partners are likely to be highly self-sufficient and will both reflect and emit a harmonious moral tone in all aspects of their life as a couple.

I suspect there may be a few outraged readers out there at this point. But I am only passing on the observations I have made of successful leaders I have known. If you want to be successful and use different guidelines to those I outline above you will, of course, do so. But remember, it's hard enough to become a great leader. Why would anybody make it harder for themselves by pairing up with a partner who is going to make success twice as hard (and far less likely)!

LINKS BETWEEN PHYSICAL AND MENTAL HEALTH

Physical and mental health are linked and are mutually interdependent. Physical health facilitates quality and speedy thinking. See, for example, Habit 7 in Covey (1989). Your mind is your main working tool as a leader. You must keep it fit with regular mental exercises. In common-sense terms, the brain works by the mechanics of oxygen, carried through your blood flow. Your body and your brain are equally dependent on these flows. It *must* make sense to ensure that the machine (of your body) is in the best possible working order.

There is a further reason for keeping yourself physically fit. What is the point to being so unfit that you cannot enjoy the fruits of your labour through pleasurable hobbies and pursuits? In many ways, both physical and mental health require the same discipline of self-control and good habits. Why not apply the same regime to all aspects of your life? Ultimately an unfit mind will show and be seen for what it is. I remember a CEO I worked with. We all knew he could never remember the details or even the main substance of what he had said even a half-hour previously. He lost the respect of his executives because he could never hold them to account for any verbal commitment. The language of leadership is verbal, not written. Later, he needed major heart surgery. He recovered some of his memory but never really worked properly again. He has now spent many years in unhappy retirement wondering what might have been if he had only looked after his body and mind.

Of course, being fit cannot safeguard you against the bad luck of ill health, but it ensures you enjoy the health that you have. It could also prevent some of the sicknesses (heart disease, ulcers, alcohol dependency and depression) that befall many leaders, as a consequence of the demands and life style of their work.

WHAT IS HAPPINESS?

Most of us have asked ourselves the perennial question 'what is it that makes us happy?' Everybody's answer will be different. In essence, most amount to something like 'being happy is mainly being busy doing a balance of all the things I enjoy doing' For many people, it also means having an important social relationship with a partner, perhaps children, family and friends. Occasionally one meets people who have never been happy, yet who appear to be leaders. I suggest they could be dangerous to themselves and their organizations. Why? Because if happiness is based upon a life balanced between social, private and business time, between serious work and leisure pursuits, between highs and lows (because life is about both), then an unhappy person is also somebody who is unbalanced. The essence of great leaders is that they retain high quality judgement at all times. The whole meaning of leadership is judgement about the balance of resources, the state of the markets, the minds of consumers, the attitudes of stakeholders and the optimal way forward.

So, it appears that good leaders have to be happy. It seems a curious requirement. But their happiness, like other people's, is about utilizing their talents and skills, energy and brain power, capacity for love and objective and wise judgement. One cannot forget that happiness usually requires a minimum of material comforts also, such as a warm home, adequate food and clothing. Leaders are also more likely to secure adequate supplies of those, too.

> So, it appears that good leaders have to be happy. It seems a curious requirement.

THE LONELINESS OF LEADERSHIP

The leadership life can be lonely. Why? Because there are very few people a leader can confide in safely and without damaging the organization. This loneliness factor is the most frequent reason for leaders employing me to help them reflect upon their problems. How does the loneliness arise? By definition, if the leader is unique and special, there are few people who will understand the organization as he or she does. Worse, there is a limited range of people able to empathize with his role and problems. Who feels like sympathizing with the person who is being paid more than anybody else in the organization to worry anyway? Furthermore, most leaders are strong characters (they need to be) and they usually dislike anything which looks or feels like whining. Anyway, there are all too many employees who would love any opportunity to fawn by 'being a good listener'. Any leader worth his or her salt would hate that. They have to put up with the fawning anyway. Presenting extra opportunities for sycophancy should be too much to bear.

There is also a continuous and real danger that data supplied to the leader is falsified to give him the impression that the results he aspires to are already being achieved. Confiding in people just gives them another opportunity to lie.

The political dimension is another major cause for loneliness. Who can a leader safely confide in? Often a spouse cannot understand the nature of the problems because they are so complex and there is a need for confidentiality. Confiding to the non-executive chair or president of the organization could be dangerous, for they are also the people who will make judgements about renewing the leader's contract or deciding his or her bonus for the year. Confiding in subordinates is equally invidious and dangerous. Information is often best disseminated on a 'need to know' basis.

How to overcome the worst aspects of leadership loneliness

Some leaders choose to trust consultants. There are some who can be trusted, although they are rare. Others choose to confide in their partner, although this does seem a heavy (and unpaid) burden, especially for those partners who have their own career to manage. Others choose carefully to trust one of the non-executive directors, hopefully one they can truly call a 'friend'. Some leaders find another leader in an unrelated field and the two confide in each other.

Another way to alleviate (rather than remove) the loneliness factor is to go on many holidays and/or short breaks. Keep things in perspective and realize that the organization will survive in your absence (it always does). Others play large quantities of golf.

One methodology which I strongly advocate, is simply to lay less emphasis on confidentiality. Most organizations put excessive emphasis on the need for secrecy. This makes leaders obsessive about it; it also certainly accentuates the sense of loneliness, because, by definition, the leader carries most secrets in his head as a consequence of his ultimate responsibility for everything in the company that is most important. When you examine them, one finds that most of the files which are marked 'confidential' are not really important or private at all and it would harm nobody if everybody knew about them. While on this subject of confidentiality, isn't it interesting how so many companies will announce their strategy to their shareholders and any of their competitors who have the intelligence to read their annual report, while not thinking it worthwhile to confide their strategy to their employees?

SUMMARY

This chapter has emphasized the need for leaders and all those preparing and managing a leadership career, to pay careful attention to the traumas of their past which cause inappropriate reactions to current events. I urge that they strive to achieve emotional balance in their lives, both for their personal happiness and the welfare of their business organization. I then lay out the bases for the need to behave as ethically at work as in one's private life, with the ever present assumption that ethics in private life are a *sine qua non*. Finally, I advocate that people who aspire to become leaders eventually should choose their partners in life carefully and with a view to the special needs that will arise as a consequence of the demands of a leadership career. Don't make it harder for yourself than it needs to be. It's already hard enough to become a great and successful leader.

RECOMMENDED READING FOR CHAPTER 3

Adair, J. (1988) *Effective Leadership*. London: Pan.

Axtell, R. E. (1991) *Gestures*. Chichester: John Wiley & Sons.

Belbin, R. M. (1991) *Management Teams*. Oxford: Butterworth Heinemann.

Belbin, M. (1993) *Team Roles at Work*. Oxford: Butterworth Heinemann.

Briggs-Myers, I. (1992) *Gifts Differing*. Palo Alto, CA.: Consulting Psychologists Press.

Chapman, E. N. (1977) *Your Attitude is Showing*. Palo Alto, CA: Science Research Associates.

Covey, S. R. (1989) *The 7 Habits of Highly Effective People*. New York: Simon & Schuster.

Ferrucci, P. (1990) *What We May Be*. London: Aquarian/Thorsons.

Goleman, D. (1996) *Emotional Intelligence*. London: Bloomsbury.

Harris, T A. (1973) *I'm OK – You're OK*. London: Pan.

Kiersey, D. and Bates, M. (1984) *Please Understand Me*. Del Mar, CA: Prometheus Nemesis Book Company.

Lewis, R. and Lowe, P. (1992) *Individual Excellence*. London Kogan Page.

McClelland, D. (1961) *The Achieving Society*. Princeton, NJ: Van Nostrand.

Peter, L. J. and Hull, R. (1979) *The Peter Principle*. London: Pan.

Schultz, C. (1955) *FIRO: A three dimensional theory of interpersonal behaviour*. New York: Holt, Rinehart and Winston.

White, R.P., Hodgson, P. and Crainer, S. (1996) *The Future of Leadership*. London: Financial Times Pitman Publishing.

Biographies of companies and leaders

Colier, P. and Horowitz, D. (1976) *The Rockefellers*. New York: Signet.

Love, J. F. (1995) *McDonald's: Behind the Arches*. New York: Bantam.

Thompson, P. (1990) *Sharing the Success*. London: Fontana.

Walton, S. (1993) *Made in America*. New York: Bantam.

THE NATURE AND DEVELOPMENT OF LEADERS

....

This chapter defines the different types of
personality which are best suited to the
leadership role. It also describes a few which
are unsuited. It makes recommendations on
how to overcome difficult or dangerous traits

....

PERSONALITY AND CHARACTER

How does *personality* differ from *character*? Personality is the more superficial manifestation of habits and surface behaviours. Most of these habits are usually accumulated during childhood by casual learning from parents and other influences, such as school teachers and friends. A individual's personality is usually what people are reacting to when they form their first impression of somebody. In some cases personality, because it is the surface or outer skin of a person's total being, can be composed of superficial elements such as physical characteristics, height or fashionable good looks. To distinguish it from character, try to think of people you have met who made a seemingly deep impression upon you at the first meeting and then, as you got to know them better, you concluded that 'there is less to them than meets the eye'.

What you saw as you began to know that person more deeply is likely to be what I am calling character. Character is the much more profound composition of the inner person. It describes the deeper aspects of their underlying psyche. It is the substance which lies within their inner core, below the shell on the surface. It is what you find when you scrape away the superficial manners and habitual responses controlled by custom. It is composed of what people deeply believe, their most strongly held life values, because it is based upon the most important influences in their lives. These will be some mixture of their basic genetically controlled instincts and the few, most concrete, elements of their developmental training, the outstanding events and values imbibed, both consciously and subconsciously, from their most important mentors. It is the 'meaning' of the inner core of the person.

How can one distinguish between character and personality? Personality, can be likened to a person's clothing rather than the body within the clothes, the wallpaper rather than the wall. Character, on the other hand, is the inner person, the sum of all their values, attitudes and experiences. A person's character represents the values which give deep meaning to their life and the qualities which govern how they take decisions about important issues. Personality is what people know about you after they have met you for a few minutes. Character is what they know about you after knowing you, or doing business with you, for ten years.

In the light of this explanation, it is apparent that it is your character that you should be trying to improve and render more robust, rather than your personality. If personality is something that can be put on and taken off, like an overcoat, you can buy the best overcoat anytime. But if you have a shabby body, both the coat and your body will always look dishevelled. You can put on a personality for a brief show, but if you have a rotten character everybody will discover the truth soon enough. I am not advocating that you ignore your personality. There are too many situations in both life and business when it is vital to make an immediately favourable impression. However, leadership is about the long term. It is about leaving permanent differences which do good to the organization for many years. Your long-term achievements will be a reflection of your character rather than your personality. Your long-term work will reflect your deeper innermost values. You can leave your children some money and it will make a shallow, surface difference to their lives. But if you succeed in inserting ethical values and the capacity for wisdom into their minds, and leave them that as an inheritance, it will enrich them forever.

> **Personality is what people know about you after they have met you for a few minutes. Character is what they know about you after knowing you, or doing business with you, for ten years.**

Two questions arise from the observations above. The first is 'can or should one's personality be aligned with one's deeper character?' The answer is that the more true that is, the better. It will ensure that fewer people can make mistakes about who you really are, at first meetings. Of course, this also implies that if you have a rotten character people will see it right away, in which case I suppose the best advice is to develop a false persona. If the two are aligned, it will mean that the values in which you deeply believe will be what you portray all the time, from first meeting to 20-year relationship. It may be summarized as 'what you see is what you get (is who you are)'.

The second question is more profound. It is, 'if one finds faults in one's character can anything be done about it?' The answer must be, surely, a resounding YES! If we believe that we cannot affect or change our character in adult life, we would all be the ill-assorted results of accidental genetics and childhood environment. Regression would be very mean indeed! I firmly believe that anyone can improve upon and change their character and the deeper value systems upon which their character is based. To do this they have to examine their roots and inner core carefully. They will need all the help they can get; it always requires ruthless honesty and candour. If you, the reader, attempt it and find important aspects of yourself that require change, be aware that it will often be painful and is thoroughly difficult to remedy. It is the behavioural equivalent of becoming left-handed, if you are naturally right-handed.

What a leader does for an organization is much more a reflection of his character than his personality because it is about the long term rather than the short. That means that a leader needs a good, stable character based upon sound ethics and values. His character should have good instincts and adopted values about 'the right thing to do in all circumstances'. When organizations interview people for any important job, they should concentrate upon discovering the inner character of the person they seek to employ. That is why it is foolish to react to the personality and the superficial aspects of a candidate that are presented in the typically short interviews that are the standard criteria for decisions about employment.

To start you on the journey of examining your own character and how it works in your favour (and for your organization) or not, you should define the type of leader you are at work. Let's examine seven key types, which are – Charismatic, Superior intelligence, Autocratic, Shepherd, Army general, Princely leader, Nature's native.

A TYPOLOGY OF LEADERS
1 Charismatic

Usually a strong personality, who is used to getting people to do things his way. Can be powerful at board level and when dealing with stakeholders.

Advantages
1 Can use charisma to get things done fast.
2 Can use charisma to persuade people that his/her strategies are optimal.

3 Adds glamour and sense of importance to all who work for them.
4 Can be used to achieve positive PR for the organization.

Disadvantages
1 Can leave people feeling manipulated.
2 Can be so strong that other charismatic people just below the leader leave the company when they don't get the top job (because he has got it) and they then lead the competition. Worse, the company is bereft of good leaders to succeed the Charismatic.
3 Can use charisma to persuade people into the wrong policies.

This style is most successful when a business needs to spend a few years taking important decisions and decisive action. Charismatic leaders persuade people fast to agree to their strategies and are the most skilled at convincing people that they can outperform their self-perception. There are disadvantages. First, they tend to outshine their subordinates. Eventually, this causes any other charismatics to depart and thus causes a void where there should be a succession plan. Second, when they get things wrong, their charisma may cause people to go along as easily with their flawed plans as their better ones. They can use their charisma to persuade people into bad plans as well as good. On the other hand they make people feel good and therefore work harder.

Can charisma be developed?

Because charisma is a manifestation of personality rather than character, it is also quite superficial. This means it is relatively easy to develop charisma by deconstructing the elements which form charisma. For example, what is it we remember about people with charisma after they leave? Often it is their clothing, their manner of speech, their presence, their hairstyle or their car. All of these are superficial attributes, most of which can be purchased or acquired with little trouble. However, if you wish to have charisma, you have to systematically acquire and accumulate these attributes for their 'differentness'. You should choose a tone of speech to be remembered by. Clothing, especially good clothing, can be acquired from the famous branded tailors. You can have your hair styled by any good hairdresser to reflect who you would like to be. A car is just another company appurtenance; it can be purchased to make a statement of show rather than of economy. Sensible leaders usually prefer the sensible option of economy. Finally, be polite. It is astonishing how many people are remembered for their rudeness rather than their effectiveness. In this case, it isn't their charisma people refer to when they recall them!

Some readers may consider this analysis of the characteristics of charisma and how to develop it somewhat shallow.

> A car is just another company appurtenance; it can be purchased to make a statement of show rather than of economy.

However, that is really all there is to charisma, when one deconstructs its elements. Charisma can be as shallow as all surface effects. It is a profound character which has a lasting effect upon people and organizations. There are many charismatics who are known to be appalling leaders. There are few people of profound and good character about whom the same is said. It is the reader's choice. Best to have both. But if you're choosing between character and charisma, go for character every time – it's harder to develop but much more worthwhile.

Some charismatics don't realize they have charisma until later in life. It is useful to be aware early if you do have it because your charisma can have startling effects upon people which, in turn, can cause unexpected results. I know one individual who emanates intelligence and power, a deadly combination. Because he didn't realize it till later life, he continuously ran into problems with people reacting to him strangely and excessively strongly. Ultimately, it stopped him doing his best because people didn't give him chances to explain himself before they reacted – his charisma was too

> The charismatic leader can persuade people to achieve objectives and strategies that they may not themselves believe in without the leader's inspiration.

strong and they feared being manipulated or overwhelmed. It's surprising that people around you are aware of your charisma but are too frightened to tell you. Sometimes charismatics are, or appear to be, shallow. If you are one of these, try to develop a brain! If you're not shallow, people will perceive it.

Charismatics are most successful in situations which require leaps of strategic vision in situations where the leadership really does know best.

The charismatic leader can persuade people to achieve objectives and strategies that they may not themselves believe in without the leader's inspiration. In these circumstances, the leader's charisma may be the only means of convincing them that they should attempt the difficult strategic vision he has set out for them.

2 Superior intelligence

The problem with leaders who rise to power on their superior intelligence is that they intimidate people without

> **Don't ever bother trying to show your intelligence, everybody will know it without your needing to show it.**

realizing it. Strangely, they often do not realize their intelligence is different from others until later in life, by which time they will have alienated many. However, leaders with an appropriate emotional intelligence will learn, when young, how to handle their intelligence. The best rule is: don't ever bother trying to show your intelligence, everybody will know it without your needing to show it.

Leaders with this mixed blessing of a style often have to spend extra time explaining things to people because people cannot keep up with their brain-processing speed and power. If they fail to realize how fast they have intuited the solution to problems while others have only just grasped the important questions, and if they don't take time to explain, they will fail to communicate their ideas to their team. The team will, in turn, be unable to implement the leader's ideas.

Advantages:
1 It creates trust and belief in the leader.
2 It works well in firms which rely on high levels of education in its employees, like the pharmaceutical industry.
3 In social situations where deference is acceptable or desirable, it can be efficacious in getting things done.

Disadvantages
1 Where the social norms find deference unacceptable, it can be problematic.
2 It can be intimidating and cause the team supporting the leader to defer to his brain power too much.

3 It can also cause people around the leader to become overwhelmed and give less than their best because of the effect of the brightness upon their thinking processes.

4 Superior intelligence can sometimes lead the organization to make wrong decisions, too, because, it over emphasizes deductive logic and not emotional empathy.

A classic leader with this style was Bob Horton, ex-leader of British Petroleum and later Railtrack. He, unfortunately, did not apply the advice above to hide his intelligence. In a company like BP, which he headed, which was full of highly intelligent, potential substitute leaders, this proved to be provocative. He was later removed, in a boardroom coup which appears to have been partially inspired by the somewhat indiscreet display of his high IQ.

Superior intelligence is most successful in businesses where there are large numbers of highly qualified or bright people. They find it easier to accept a superior intelligence leader. Having invested so much of their lives in achieving qualifications, they tend to develop an exaggerated respect for brain power as contrasted to the emotional intelligence that, I argue, is so much more important for leaders than plain IQ.

3 Autocratic

The autocratic style is usually considered not an appropriate style for the late 20th century. However, appearing to be, or actually being, autocratic tends to be a feature of personality. Given its unsuitability for modern work practices, I advocate adapting the style only under the most extreme circumstances, when the organization and its circumstances demand. There are some situations when autocracy really is the most suitable style for the business situation. For example, whenever one is in a rapid turn-round to save a business, or in a rapid market growth environment, trying to grab market share at the start of an industry, during its most competitive phases.

Advantages
1 It wastes little time.

2 It is attractive to other autocratic types.

3 It is often suited to sales-led organizations where the sales force merely requires direction.

4 It can be great in war time or when there's a *burning platform** issue.

Disadvantages

1 It annoys intelligent people who don't like taking orders.

2 It is inadequate when dealing with complex strategic situations.

3 It fails to exploit the brains of the best people in the organization.

4 It creates a tendency in the leader to believe in his own infallibility.

5 It creates an atmosphere with low levels of feedback.

6 Too many inadequate managers copy the style causing the business itself to take on counterproductive styles and attributes which, in turn, inhibit the recruitment of the right sort of staff.

The autocratic style is most successful in a crisis, when an organization has to change rapidly, whether growing or turning itself from decline to growth. It can also be useful during periods of highly competitive battle for market share, when new products are battling it out in the market-place.

4 Shepherd

The shepherd style is most akin, in its behaviour patterns, to the shepherd who tends his flock. This type of leader treats his or her employees, customers and other stakeholders with care and solicitude. This leader tends to push rather than pull and allows people time to come alongside the leader's point of view. The shepherd tends to be a gentle but strong soul, who usually understands people very well and attracts much love and devotion from the staff and personnel in general. They are usually spoken of in terms such as 'strong but gentle' and 'dependable'.

---

* The phrase burning platform refers to situations such as those on an oil rig when the platform is on fire and every decision has to be taken immediately and with dire consequences if the decision is wrong.

Advantages
1 Builds a resilient business.
2 Safe and sound.
3 Unlikely to be surprised by changes in the market or catastrophe.
4 Admired leader, although difficult to copy.

Disadvantages
1 Not good in situations requiring very fast reactions.
2 Tends to lose intuitive, fast reacting subordinates who get impatient.
3 Can miss market opportunities because takes too long to react.
4 Poses particular difficulties for market analysts and stockbrokers who tend to work in much shorter time-frames than this kind of leader.

This style is most successful when the organization needs steady leadership for a relatively calm period. It is most endangered when there is a crisis or a prolonged battle for intellectual supremacy (for example, the computer software industry) or when the organization contains many highly qualified people who like to feel they are in an intellectual hot house. This leader does not represent that style well.

5 Army general

This style follows the classical army analogy. The army general type of leader, like his army counterpart, tries to set great examples but expects his people to follow his commands unquestioningly. They assume obedience and followership. They exude an air of having a total grasp of the situation and exhibit supreme confidence that their solutions and explanations are right, appropriate and need not be questioned. They differ from the autocrat style because their belief in their right to obedience comes from confidence in their own decisions and opinions rather than an innate belief in their superiority and right to lead. Their command style does not come from a need to order people, nor an inability to listen to others, but from self-confidence in their right to lead and ability to do so. This style is often admired because it allows others to encapsulate their own sense of destiny. In the same way that many lower ranks in the armed forces accept their positions unquestioningly (especially after suitable training), so also do the subordinates of this style of leader. Of course, those who can't stand it, disappear fast enough. However, this style of leadership is rarely questioned and easily obeyed. Usually the general is a decent sort, who has a good sense of community and social values of a conservative nature.

Advantages
1 People find him easy to follow and want to obey.
2 Tends to specialize in mature industries.
3 Usually a good, precise, and clear communicator, so all stakeholders know what they must do to be successful and when.
4 Creates a sense of fairness and gives *raison d'être* to staff.
5 Usually a great exponent of the art of helicoptering (*see* Chapter 5).
6 Dependable and reliable – predicted results can be banked.

Disadvantages
1 Can be slow to react to catastrophe.
2 Often doesn't understand people who don't share their sense of duty.
3 May be unattractive to young, brash or extremely bright potential leaders.
4 Doesn't easily admit wrong thinking.
5 Can be pompous and bad at listening.
6 Sometimes bad-tempered.

This type of leadership is most successful defending a dominant or leadership position in the market. The army general, like his counterpart in real armies, spends much of his time preparing for battles and wars which, hopefully, won't take place. Similarly, the army general leadership style is most successful preventing battles and wars, by ensuring the competition believe they cannot win, so it is not worth attacking.

6 Princely leader

The princely leader is seen as a natural aristocrat. He or she appears to have been born to lead and emanates a natural style of leadership, with an easy sense of knowing the right thing to do and when. This type of leader is attractive and seigneurial, exuding a sense of destiny and a natural right to be the leader, but can be unapproachable. This serves to facilitate a preference to be carefully selective about whom he or she talks to, meets or takes data from. This can be useful, in terms of managing his or her time, but can lead to problems with subordinates or business associates who find the style annoying or who are easily intimidated. They tend to stay away from this type and therefore deprive him or her of their insights (while simultaneously depriving themselves of the opportunity to be noticed and rewarded for good work).

Advantages
1 Highly attractive to many followers and easy to work for.
2 Finds time to listen and learn from others (if they seem worth listening to).
3 Makes people proud to be in his or her camp.
4 Seems such a natural leader that it prevents many from feeling that they could do the job just as easily.
5 People find it easy to obey, (therefore, little time wasted questioning his or her decisions).

Disadvantages
1 Natural egalitarians resent this style of leadership and either leave or don't join.
2 Can lead to unquestioning loyalty which doesn't ask enough questions.
3 Sometimes a little unintelligent.
4 Suited to industries with *ostentatious consumption** type goods or monopolistic tendencies; this can have unfortunate consequences with regulators. This style seems to be particularly favoured by both Sotheby's and Christies, the two originally British auction businesses which dominate the international auction industry.

The princely leader is most successful in long-established businesses which have powerful brands and dependable market share. They excel at regal leadership, taking finely calculated decisions to move the ocean liner a few degrees to port or starboard. They are at their most vulnerable when under attack, because they find it hard to respond with alacrity. They are

---

* Ostentatious consumption goods are articles which people buy for the opportunity this gives them to demonstrate their wealth to others, such as paintings, diamond rings, fur coats or luxurious cars.

used to having their positions by right and don't know how to cope with upstarts who attack them; their natural dignity erodes fast and they either become bewildered or they freeze.

7 Nature's native

The nature's native leader is one who always looks comfortable in the leading position. He conducts himself in the leadership role as if it was all he was ever meant to do. A typical leader with this style would be Bob Bauman, Tony Blair or President John Kennedy. They look as if leadership is what they were born to do. People who work for these nature's native leaders couldn't imagine having them as a subordinate. They look like they always were leaders; they do it without thinking. They don't panic, they use the helicopter tool (Chapter 5) with ease, they appear rarely strained and then not so that ordinary mortals would notice. They make 'nominal leaders' feel as inadequate as they frequently are. They are envied for the naturalness of their gifts and qualities of leadership, but are rarely resented – they don't excite that type of shallow response in people who work with and for them.

Advantages
1 Can take leadership role very young and be accepted.
2 Never feels or looks uncomfortable.
3 Always looks like they know what to do in any situation (and usually does).
4 Tends to have a multitude of behavioural styles and thinking patterns, depending what is required in any situation or stage in the economic cycle.
5 Usually extremely intelligent and wise and able to take complex decisions with easy facility.

Disadvantages
1 It all looks so easy, it seems unfair.
2 Can appear to be more style than substance.
3 So bright that it takes followers much concentration to understand the complexity and cleverness of their strategic insights.
4 One is never sure they are pleased with somebody's efforts because their

own achievements seem so natural, they assume it is equally easy for others, too.

5 They forget to say 'thank you'.

Nature's natives are effective under most circumstances. However, they excel in large-scale, multinational or global organizations, because their style transcends local or national, culturally narrow behaviour and enables them to fit into most nationalities and cultures. Leaders of businesses such as Unilever often match this style. Indeed, a business which would be best led by a leader with this style would be Shell, the global energy business, but in recent years this has not been the case. This would explain how the leadership of Shell misinterpreted public reaction all around the world to their proposal for disposal of a redundant oil rig in an environmentally unacceptable method of sinking it in the ocean. A truly cosmopolitan leadership, acting as nature's natives would never have miscalculated the potential public reaction so wrongly.

Summary of leadership styles

The reason for setting out lists of styles is to guide readers who are developing their own style as they mature and become leaders in their own right. It may be that their personal style is an amalgam of some or all of the above. Leadership styles should, by definition, be idiosyncratic; leaders need to create a fresh, individual style of their own. However, the list of styles laid out above can act as a guide to the range that can be seen in organizations and the effect they can have, for good and bad, upon their followers. There is no style which does not have some unfortunate consequences. That is also a reminder that the perfect leader has not yet been born. It also leads to the topic of leaders' analysis of themselves and the underlying reasons they have their particular personal style with its various effects upon their subordinates. Why is it that certain leaders choose particular styles as their vehicle for leadership? How much of the choice is a free one and how much is controlled by the givens of their personality and character traits? I discuss the Belbin teamskills analytical tool below, as well as the more profound FIRO-B analysis of fundamental behavioural traits. In Table 4.1, I mention a whole range of other instruments which can be used. Where

Table 4.1 Summary of leadership styles

Style	Best situation	Worst situation	Comments
Charismatic	Moments of great strategic leaps forward	Steady state, when quality succession planning is preferable	Charismatic leaders drive out other types of quality people
Superior intelligence	Businesses which employ many bright and well qualified people	Marketplace fights for low value, highly branded, popular products	Brains admire other brains, usually. Other leaders with more empathetic qualities, don't value this style
Autocratic	Great in a crisis because they don't feel the need to ask too many questions	Inappropriate when work force is well educated and highly qualified	Works well in many situations. Particularly effective in the UK, where people accept class differences easily
Shepherd	Excellent in a steady state business	Can panic in a crisis or situations needing fast reactions	Great in gilt-edged stocks
Army general	Great when preparing for war	Not necessarily great in the heat of battle	Usually better at preparation than finishing. Relies on not needing to finish because everybody thinks their preparation is so good, they will win the battle
Princely leader	Long established businesses with leading brands	Not effective leading businesses with mass demand, such as groceries	A dangerous style for the business because they are hard to remove and don't easily recognize when they are no longer appropriate
Nature's native	Good in most circumstances, especially well-branded global businesses	Organizations which are heavily sales led	Probably the most effective all-round style. They make everybody feel better about going to work – and they keep the owners happy

readers find they are deeply fascinated by any particular one, they can probably obtain details of it through local trainers. It is not possible to offer the detailed questionnaires in this book, because in most cases they are protected by the holders of copyright.

> **Why is it that certain leaders choose particular styles as their vehicle for leadership? How much of the choice is a free one and how much is controlled by the givens of their personality and character traits?**

USE OF PSYCHOMETRIC ANALYSES

Psychometric analytical tools can be most efficacious when trying to analyze one's own or others' personalities and characters. Obviously some are more profound than others. The Belbin teamskills test, for example, is useful but gives no profound insight into character. Rather it tends to inform the user of the current preoccupations and preferences of the recipient at any point in time when the test is administered. Another great value of psychometric testing is as a back-up to intuition. It can confirm impressions given during interviews or when working alongside somebody, particularly if there are traits which one cannot explain to oneself but which give cause for concern. They are also useful when starting discussions on important topics, about individuals in their work behaviour. Their use tends to liberate a respondent and their facilitator and creates the right atmosphere to talk about sometimes difficult and intimate subjects. Their use can, above all, gets you into interesting and revealing discussions at a fast pace. Psychometric testing can also give warnings and hints about the sadder or more difficult aspects of people's characters and behaviour, which can then be followed up with referees and other holders of information.

Psychometric tests can be used to facilitate the creation of a balanced executive team or board of directors. When the results from these tests are disseminated through the business or exchanged with key players in the organization, it can give all the key executives a vocabulary on feeling and thinking styles, which can be important, later, when working together in emergencies or even more mundane organizational processes. Finally, when used sensitively, psychometric tests can provide major clues on how to handle difficult executives and, especially, how to maximize their individual contribution, as well as that of the whole team.

Table 4.2 Use of psychometric analyses: which test gives the
appropriate insight?

Insight required	Test recommended
Preferred team behaviours	Belbin teamskills test
Thinking style	Myers-Briggs Types Indicator
Thinking skills	Watson-Glaser
Judgement skills	Watson-Glaser
Temperament	Myers-Briggs Types Indicator
Social skills	FIRO-B
Leadership drive	FIRO-B
Capacity for accepting guidance	FIRO-B
Personal emotional maturity	FIRO-B
Need for interaction with others	FIRO-B
Leadership style	FIRO-B
Use of different situational leadership styles	LEAD (Hersey and Blanchard)
Levels and types of conflict style	Thomas Kilman Conflict Mode
Use of political behaviours	Machievelli scale
Motivations for work	Hunt work-interest schedule

Uses and warnings about use of selected psychometric tests

Many of these tests are under copyright control. Also, it is not usually the work of leaders to get involved in administering such tests. I have included detailed descriptions of one or two in this book because they can be used to achieve special insights into the deeper nature of the leaders and subordinates. The Belbin teamskills test, dealt with below, is one favourite. Another is the FIRO-B Behaviour Questionnaire, which is also discussed later in this chapter.

1 Myers-Briggs Types Indicator

The Myers-Briggs Types Indicator is one of the most commonly applied tests in the business world. It describes a respondent's personality on four axes. They are:

- introversion/extroversion
- sensing/intuition
- thinking/feeling
- judgement/perception.

The Myers-Briggs Types Indicator is highly esteemed by its practitioners and I have seen it used to great effect by leaders to gain insights into some of their key executives. Many use it as part of their selection criteria for new employees at senior level. However, I have some reservations about it (which do not diminish its general merit). First, its practitioners tend to use too much mumbo-jumbo when they talk to each other and their respondents. Occasionally it is used in too technical a manner, so that you cannot see the wood from the trees. It can be confusing to some respondents because it has so many types they find it hard to see what is, and what is not useful, when they examine their results or those of their people. Nevertheless, it does help respondents to understand the full range of human behaviour and to have greater sympathy with people who have entirely different temperaments to themselves.

2 The FIRO-B: introduction and explanation

The FIRO-B questionnaire is closely based upon the work of Jung and was developed by W. C. Schultz (*see* Schultz 1955). The letters stand for Fundamental Interpersonal Relations Orientation-Behaviour. It examines the way a person typically acts with other people. This information can be helpful whatever work settings you are thinking about, especially when you combine this knowledge with information about your interests, skills and values. When you work in situations where your natural tendencies are in harmony with the job, you are happier, you do better work, and have more of a competitive edge.

The FIRO-B questionnaire helps you become more aware of your interpersonal behaviours and habits. When aware of these behaviour patterns, you can adjust your behaviour where it might cause distortions in people's reactions to you. The FIRO-B gives you information about yourself on three types of work behaviour, *Inclusion*, *Control*, and *Affection*. Each dimension describes both how much you express to others and compares it to how much you need yourself. (Control is sometimes better thought of as 'how much control you want over others compared to how much control you will accept from others'.) The meaning of the three dimensions is described below:

Inclusion. This refers to one's social skills, the ability to get on with people. Like all the FIRO-B dimensions, it is divided into how much one *expresses to* others and how much one *wants from* other people. *Inclusion expressed* refers to the social skills you use to let people around feel you are including them; *inclusion wanted* refers to how much you really want to spend time with people other than the necessary minimum. Inclusion is a useful indicator of whether there is too large a differential between a person's social skills and their need to be alone. If they have too low a score on inclusion expressed it also warns that they may lack the social skills that are necessary for leadership.

Control. This relates mainly to leadership behaviour. *Control expressed* describes how much control you like to exert over others; *control wanted* describes how much control you are able to accept from others. Control can help indicate when a leader resembles what I have called a 'nominal leader'. Such leaders often exhibit an excessive need to control others, accompanied by an inability to accept control from anybody else. This can be dangerous because even the most powerful leader is never completely free from control. If one cannot accept this truth it demonstrates a lack of sense of reality. High-control-expressed people also tend to try to achieve excessively high objectives or offer them to their chair person or the market analysts. They are then hoist on the petard of their excessively high ambitions for the business; they either fail to deliver results (and lose their job) or they deliver them with excessive cost to the organization (in people and resource terms), thus making it harder to deliver reasonable expectations in the future.

Affection. This relates to deep, rather than superficial, personal relationships. *Affection expressed* describes how much affection you express to other people; *affection wanted* describes how much affection you want from others. Some leaders, who exhibit a low need for affection, may have an unbalanced attitude to social life. Sometimes this test indicates an excessive need for affection from others. This could be indicative of a level of insecurity and dependency which could be problematic for a leader. Significantly, on this scale, very low scores on both affection wanted and given could be a signal of a sadly lost soul. I always try to investigate these cases when I discover them. There is nearly always a serious problem underlying such results.

FIRO-B also gives two other indications which are relevant and important to leadership skills. One is an interpersonal score (IPS), which is the degree to which a person prefers more or less human interaction (similar to the Myers-Briggs introversion/extroversion axis). The other is the expression of anger (EAS) score, which is sometimes more easily understood as a 'frustration score'. It indicates how quickly you become frustrated or angry with people. When the anger scores are too high, it usually indicates that the respondent's anger is causing people around them to avoid them. They become increasingly isolated and fail to get feedback from their staff, thus rendering themselves less effective. If their anger scores are too low, the respondent may fail to give sufficient feedback to their subordinates (because they are uncomfortable when giving clear signals of dissatisfaction to people).

FIRO-B is a remarkably accurate gauge of how a person behaves at work. When used by the best practitioners, it can deliver a powerful insight into how you are perceived at work. It is most useful in analyzing respondents' social skills, their need to control people and their levels of anger.

3 The Belbin Teamskills Test

For the greater part of a leadership career, leaders will be in situations which require them to be part of a team effort. These will be times when the leader's capacity for individuality and seeing the world differently will not only be superfluous, but could even get in the way of the team's need to achieve its objectives. It is necessary for a leader to know, under these circumstances, what their own teamskills may be.

There are many questionnaires designed to give you feedback on how you behave in a team situation. One of the best known is the Belbin Self

Perception Inventory. It is available freely from Dr Mereith Belbin's book, *Management Teams* (Belbin 1981).

The essence of Dr Belbin's work is that no single individual can combine in themselves all the qualities it takes to accomplish the total corporate role. A team of individuals can. This is why it is not the individual but the team that is the instrument of sustained and enduring success in management (but not in leadership). The implication is that, while not ignoring or neglecting the individual, we should devote far more thought to teams, their selection, development and training and, above all, to their psychology, motivation, composition and behaviour. The trouble is that, by comparison with our knowledge of individual psychology, our knowledge of what makes teams successful is tiny. Dr Belbin's crucial contribution is the fact that all members of a management team have a dual role. The first role, the functional one, is obvious; a manager belongs to the team because he is an accountant or production engineer or regional service manager or group marketing executive, or whatever. We also know, however, that certain people in a team always come up with bright ideas, or get decisions finalized or tasks allocated. These people are likely to show the same characteristics whatever team they belong to.

Dr Belbin believes there are eight characteristic *team* roles that crop up repeatedly. It follows that if one can list all the different contributing types that are needed in a team to balance each other, one may have some of the clues to creating a perfect team. It is these enduring, characteristic team roles that have been the subject of Dr Belbin's research. He has isolated and identified just eight roles as the only ones necessary to create a full set of team members. They are: Company worker, Chair person, Shaper, Plant, Resource investigator, Monitor evaluator, Team worker, Completer finisher. Below is a very brief summary of the traits and meaning of each of these:

> No single individual can combine in themselves all the qualities it takes to accomplish the total corporate role. A team of individuals can. This is why it is not the individual but the team that is the instrument of sustained and enduring success in management (but not in leadership).

The Company worker: A person who, once given a decision, will produce a list or schedule.

The Chair: A person who clarifies the group's objectives and sets its agenda. They are stable, dominant, extrovert and tend to preside over the team and co-ordinate its efforts to meet goals and targets.

The Shaper: Shapers are only reassured by the task and by results. Their results-driven behaviour has a compulsive quality.

The Plant: This person is usually the team's source of original ideas, suggestions and proposals. They tend to be dominant with a very high IQ and are usually introvert.

The Resource investigator: These people make friends easily and have masses of outside contacts. They are stable, dominant and extrovert. They bring in ideas for solutions – but, unlike the Plant, they are borrowed ideas, not original ones.

The Monitor evaluator: These people mull things over and give objective judgements. They usually have a high IQ, as well as being stable and introvert. They often appear to be rather a cold fish.

The Team worker may be better thought of as the team friend. This person promotes unity and harmony and counterbalances friction and discord (often caused by the Shaper, pushing to get the task completed.

The Completer finisher is a compulsive meeter of deadlines and fulfiller of schedules, with a tendency to be anxious and introvert, worrying constantly about what might go wrong.

A summary of the Belbin team analysis tool

The theory behind the Belbin self perception inventory questionnaire says that the Company worker will schedule the work, the Shaper will drive the team compulsively towards the result; the Chair will ensure that everybody in the team is used properly; the Plant will come up with original ideas to solve the problem; the Resource investigator will get ideas from others if the Plant's ideas are not working; the Team worker will make the team feel better when it is not making any headway, which the Monitor

> **When the team operates in areas of rapid change in the workforce, manufacturing new products, developing emerging markets or de-scaling costs, where there is competition pressure and need for quick decision and action, then having all the different team skills available becomes of paramount importance.**

evaluator will bluntly tell the team about; the Completer finisher will ensure that the team actually carries out the task as scheduled.

The question then arises, what happens if you have fewer than eight people? The answer is that everybody has secondary team roles, which are the team skills that are second (and occasionally third) highest in their results. Thus they can double up when necessary and perform more than one function.

The building of teams by balancing the team roles is not of the same importance to every kind of operation. It is far less significant, for instance, for a group whose principal role is to supervise a more or less steady and continuous process without much change over the years and with no great need for alteration or innovation. On the other hand, when the team operates in areas of rapid change in the workforce, manufacturing new products, developing emerging markets or de-scaling costs, where there is competition pressure and need for quick decision and action, then having all the different team skills available becomes of paramount importance.

Teams are important. But great leaders get things right, in spite of their poor teams – or they improve the team. The case below tries to put things into perspective This man had the training – he even had the brains but not the insight into his own strengths and weaknesses to know what he needed his team to be – to make him what he needed to become.

Case Study 4.1

TEAMS CAN LOSE BUSINESSES

I worked for many years with a bright and extremely intellectual leader. We first became acquainted when I was his tutor on a managing director's programme he was attending. This man had a large capacity for intellectual analysis of most business problems. Unfortunately, this was not accompanied with skills for relating at a human level with his subordinates at work. This doubt was recorded and explained why his promotion to managing director status came many years later than he expected. When he had been in the post about a year he telephoned me to tell me that his new board of directors were not really knitting as a team. Could I help? Unfortunately, by the time he called me in, he had already changed most members of his team. He had new directors of marketing, information technology and was about to appoint a fresh finance director. I asked him what criteria he had used to compose his team? He responded 'They are the most thoroughly intellectual group of people I could have wanted. Every one of them has a high IQ.' I pointed out that he, as MD, had enough brain power and IQ for any team. What he needed from his people was empathy and emotional insight into the feelings running around the firm and its customers. But it was too late; the new people were in position. A year later he and his board decided to change the firm's technology. It was an intellectually daring and exciting challenge. The change went catastrophically wrong when the workers in the company proved unable to change their work habits. The firm started to lose money at the rate of 10 per cent of total revenue. He and his board were all asked to leave the business.

WHAT TO DO ABOUT ONE'S PERSONALITY

What do you do when the results of one of these psychometric tests demonstrates to you that you are not as perfect as you first perceived yourself to be? Firstly, breathe a sigh of relief. The perfect human being is somebody we are all ready to hate! But then realize that these tests are there to help you get an insight into yourself and the effect of your personality and preferred way of dealing with people. In other words, it's rare

> **You need to ask yourself whether you may be paying too high a price for the rewards you think you are getting.**

that you will discover something about yourself that is completely new. Rather it will remind you of traits and tendencies that you have stopped paying attention to. Further, it will remind you how others see you – often a salutary lesson. Finally, psychometric tests can give you an agenda for change, especially when you are reminded that there can be severe emotional prices to pay for the leadership life you have chosen. You need to ask yourself whether you may be paying too high a price for the rewards you think you are getting. I often think that the most valuable use of psychometric exercises is to tell you *what you cannot do* and *what you are lacking*. This should let you know what you need from others, in order to become a truly great leader.

AN EXTRA WORKING TOOL FOR LEADERS: THE AGGREGATED USE OF PSYCHOMETRICS

Over the past 20 years I have developed methods for aggregating the results of the psychometric tests of complete executive teams which help my clients (leaders of large corporations in the main) to gain an insight into the general climate and temperament of the senior echelons of their business. These aggregated test results can sometimes give a profound and accurate insight into the employees' cultural spirit. In many ways, these aggregations may contain a greater quality of accuracy about the generality of the group than they can give truth about any individual alone. I set out below an example of the aggregates of one set of FIRO-B results that give an insight into the value and application of such an aggregation. When psychometric results are used in this manner, they become another tool for the analysis of the corporate culture or, at least, that of the cadres of executives one is examining.

Table 4.3 Aggregated FIRO-B results of leaders in a fast growth company

Inclusion expressed	Inclusion wanted	Control expressed	Control wanted	Affection expressed	Affection wanted	Inter-personal score	Expression of anger
3	2	7	2	3	7	24	28L
6	5	5	1	3	3	23	77H
4	0	5	2	3	5	17	88H
3	1	7	2	0	2	15	91H
4	0	7	1	3	0	15	100H
5	2	8	1	5	4	25	58M
7	7	5	6	8	6	39	33L
6	5	7	5	3	4	30	47L
5	3	2	2	3	3	18	85H
2	0	9	4	2	1	18	96H
5	0	6	3	2	3	19	88H
						Scale range 0–54	Scale = 0–100 H = high = 24% M = Medium = 30% L = Low = 46%
		These scores range from 0 to 9					

I will try to take you through an analysis of the group displayed. They are the senior executives and the managing directors of a quoted Footsie 250 company. First examine the Inclusion expressed column. The maximum theoretical score for any respondent would be 9. The highest actual score is 7, but most scored 4, 5 or 6. This indicates a relatively well balanced group of people with average social skills. However, when we examine their Inclusion wanted scores, we see most of the scores are considerably below those in the expressed column, including several who score zero. This indicates that although people in this group can express themselves well in terms of inclusion they do not actually, as a group, really want much social intercourse at all. To paraphrase, they all issue invitations to the Xmas party but none of them intends to turn up! You can imagine the type of social tension this can place upon the organization and themselves as a group. They can appear to be hypocritical, insincere and, simply, 'never there!'

Now examine the Control expressed (control wanted *over others*) column. The maximum score per individual is, again, 9. Notice how many score 5 or more, with many 7s, 8s or 9s. This indicates a fairly high need to exercise control over others, almost to the point of excess. Compare this to the Control wanted (*from others*) column. The contrast is stark. Now the same people say they want almost no control over themselves from anybody. People who achieve scores such as these are known as Mission Impossible type personalities because they are driven to ever greater control and ever higher levels of aspiration, knowing no rational achievement behaviour boundaries and often driving their people to distraction.

There are no normal groups.

When I explained these scores to the chief executive, he exclaimed, 'Now I understand why I feel I can never control them! How will I ever cope?' Fortunately, there was an answer. This business was trying to build an infrastructure for a new, emerging market. It had to beat the competition to get its infrastructure built first. There was a fair chance that which ever company came second would become victim to a takeover by the winner. In fact, this team of Mission Impossible types was just the right team for the task, provided that they were motivated. I recommended always giving them more difficult objectives and more tasks than most rational executives would choose to cope with. Why? Firstly because Mission Impossible types need to achieve excessively, to compensate for a deeply felt self perception of inadequacy. They always take on too much and continuously try to prove themselves against impossible odds. Furthermore, when I saw their Expression of anger column I noticed that 7 out of 11 had a high anger score. A normal expectation would have been 24 per cent rather than the 64 per cent who actually manifested high anger scores. It could only be by keeping them extremely busy that this group could be prevented from working themselves and their subordinates to a state of nervous and cowed exhaustion. If and when they were to achieve their objectives, they would all then turn upon each other and destroy the business!

SUMMARY

There are no normal groups. But every group about whom I have assembled aggregations demonstrated tendencies which made their group behaviour more predictable and also reflected (and affected) their company culture. Such aggregations can give leaders a valuable tool with which to decide how to lead their key executives. They should also be ready to take advantage of any personal insights such psychometric scoring gives into the nature of the individuals in their teams, as well as their own personality traits and their effects upon others.

A CHALLENGE

Using the information about the two tests described in detail in this book, complete the following questionnaire, which is an amalgam of the concepts of the Belbin and FIRO-B questionnaires. When you have completed it think about the implications of the questions and your score, what they mean and what they tell you about your own personality traits. What are the best and the worst features of your own behavioural habits? What should you do about them? Try to draw up a plan to obviate the worst effects of the key three weaknesses you perceive in yourself. Set yourself a target date by which you will have made some headway in combating the worst effects of these weaknesses upon your leadership style and your effectiveness at work. Keep a timetable. When you achieve the first three goals, set three more. Make it a habit of self-improvement.

Questionnaire 4.1
A SELF-ASSESSMENT QUESTIONNAIRE
USING CONCEPTS FROM THE FIRO-B, BELBIN AND MYERS-BRIGGS QUESTIONNAIRES

Study the statements, and then assess yourself on a scale of 1–10 where 1–3 means you consider you do it very little, 4–7 means you do it moderately and 8–10 means you do it a lot. Then apply the multiplier and put the final score in the last column.

Statement	Your score	Multiplier	Final score
1 When confronted with a problem or a decision your first instinct is to produce a list or schedule.		x4	
2 When you attend a meeting with a group of people, you tend to be the person who clarifies the group's objectives and sets its agenda. You enjoy co-ordinating the team's efforts to meet goals and targets.		x7	
3 You tend to focus strongly on achieving each of your tasks and you feel reassured mainly by results. This is a strong driver of how you work.		x3	
4 When meeting with a group of people, trying to solve a problem, you tend to be the person who comes up with original ideas, suggestions and proposals. However, you sometimes find it hard to get your ideas across.		x1	
5 You make freinds easily and have masses of outside contacts. You like people and find it easy to get them to give you information.		x3	
6 You like to mull things over and give people objective truth. You usually get it right, but you find quite often, people don't appreciate you when you do.		x7	
7 You enjoy being a friend to all members of your team. You believe it is your duty to promote unity and harmony and counterbalance the atmosphere caused when others are driving the team hard.		x1	
8 When the rest of the team is pleased that it has completed a task, you feel it is a			

duty to remind them they have failed to complete important details. Then you nag them to finish the job properly.	x2	
9 You have relatively easy social skills and get on well with people. They feel you want them in your team.	x5	
10 Having given your time to people at work, when you've completed your day, you prefer to keep further social interaction to the necessary minimum.	x2	
11 As a leader, you feel a strong need, because of your ability, to be in charge of others.	x5	
12 Although you are the leader, you feel no problem in letting others guide you, whether they are above, below or at the same level as you, in the organization, hierarchy.	x3	
13 You find it easy to express genuine, close friendship to people in the organization, as well as outside the business.	x3	
14 You like people to express their genuine, close friendship feelings to you, whether within or outside the business.	x2	
15 In an average week, you need a fair proportion of time on your own, to recharge your mental batteries.	x2	
16 You have the capacity to find all types of people easy to work with and interesting, no matter their skills or style.	x4	
Total your final score		

Evaluation

0–99	Possibly not destined for leadership
100–199	Potential competence but needs lots of work
200–249	Competence beginning
250–299	High level of competence or, possibly, high drive with less competence
300–349	Potential to be a fine leader
350–399	Probably already a fine leader
400–449	Moving close to top levels in major corporation
450–499	Destined for top levels in major corporation
500 upward	Should already be leading a large organization

How to increase levels of self-control

Self-control is the essence of becoming a great leader, because it is only by the exercise of massive self-control that you can stay calm enough to continuously assess all the data coming at you from many different directions and at many different levels, from the shrill to the excessively quiet. It is by exercising power over one's impulses that you can make balanced, rather than emotional judgements that will maximize the benefits to the organization from your decisions. Furthermore, because great leaders want success for themselves and their organization, they will do whatever it takes to get it right. If that means learning to exercise vast self-control, that is what they will do.

When leaders tell me how hard they find it to learn to exercise total self-control I ask them to consider the price they will pay, personally, if they fail. If, eventually, they do not reach the level in the organization that their leadership skills deserve, they will pay the price of not having appropriate outlets for their intellect and energy. Without the organizational position and the complex problems and tasks that leadership roles confer, the special type of intellect and energy that leaders have can turn from a talent to a burden. It can become utterly soul-destroying to have inadequate uses for a fine brain and high energy. Most leaders understand this force within themselves. They are right to worry more about the loss of outlets for their brain-power and energy than the loss of office, status or income.

> **When leaders tell me how hard they find it to learn to exercise total self-control I ask them to consider the price they will pay, personally, if they fail.**

There is another factor in their thinking. People of quality are often honest with themselves. They know they would not be able to avoid their own assessment of themselves at the end of their career. They would have to face the possibility that, if they had exercised more self-control, they would have had a more enjoyable and useful career.

So, how do you learn to exercise the necessary self-control? First you have to remember continuously, how much you need the work because it fulfils you. It's a great discipline. Use the helicopter tool, alongside the time horizon machine (Chapter 5), to remain dispassionate and to ensure you get your reactions to events into perspective. Never lose your common sense. It's a great litmus test of what your key constituents, customers and staff will accept in your decisions about the business.

Based on the leaders I have observed, it's also a great idea to have an active social life apart from your business life. Take all the holidays you are allocated by your terms and conditions of employment; build in lots of short breaks, too. Above all, give yourself enough time to sort any major personal problems. They don't go away just because an important leader is neglecting them rather than one of your subordinates – who may have more time to sort their problems – and have a happier life as a result.

Finally, remember that, if you *are* one of the gifted few destined to be a great leader, you need to exercise self-control and force yourself to change your personality and behaviour to fit the needs of your opportunities. If you ever feel like giving up, (and it is not a characteristic of leaders to do so) remember that your brain power and energy is not going to go away. You will always have your talent, ability, drive and energy. If you do not succeed in making the necessary changes now, what are you going to do when you are 50 or 55? Where will you find the outlets for your drive and energy? How much worse will be your frustration in not having fulfilled your destiny because you didn't control your behaviour, change your attitudes and take total possession of yourself. When you reach 60, how will you forgive yourself for not having made the effort and for allowing your future to get behind you rather than remain in front?

Unfavourable indicators for leaders

A lack of intelligence can be a serious problem! Although this sounds facetious, it is meant seriously. I have observed many nominal leaders who have reached top leadership jobs through the exercise of will power and determination but with a serious shortfall of the necessary grey matter it takes to do the job. A lack of what I have described elsewhere in this book as emotional intelligence is an even more serious problem. This causes a lack of insight into other people and possibly a lack of understanding of oneself – hazardous blind spots for any leader. Similarly, if a leader's emotional well-being leads to a constitutional lack of independence, this can be a menace to themselves and their organization. The symptoms displayed may be excessive anger or, possibly, a highly unbalanced life. The manifestations at work are likely to be an excessive need to control everything in sight, matched by an inability to take correct decisions. Sometimes this will be disguised by the leader requiring subordinates to amass large amounts of data to help them avoid the need to take what they know will be a wrong decision; or they get their subordinates to take responsibility for it themselves. Immature emotional intelligence may lead to an excessive need to be admired or loved. It is only equalled by the possible matching defect of having an insufficient need to be liked. An individual who does not need love doesn't need people enough to be in an organization composed of humans.

> **A lack of intelligence can be a serious problem!**

An excess of charisma can also be a problem, because, as I explained above, high levels of charisma sometimes disguise a lack of brain power. Too little charisma, on the other hand, might make a leader so boring that nobody will want to work for them. Excessive introspection can also be difficult, whether caused by shyness or social awkwardness, but is only important where it affects their self-perception.

Excessive fawning fathers' foolishness

As leaders move up the corporate ladder, people surrounding them become aware of the inevitability of their eventual occupation of a top position. This creates an interesting phenomenon, as they begin to accumulate power. Power exerts a strong attraction on people. They begin to tell the rising leader what they think the leader wants to hear. They start to fawn upon him or her in subtle ways. The leader becomes accustomed to it. The less aware of the fawning a leader becomes, the less useful a leader they will be.

Why are so many employees attracted to the power positions of leaders that they give less than honest views of the truth, when speaking to them? The answer lies in their desire to influence the leader and to achieve their personal objectives for the business. They may believe their personal aims for the business are also in the organization's best interests. Influence over the leader gives subordinates the power to influence the whole organization. Power is infectious and everybody wants to deliver what they think is best for the business. In addition, leaders are often attractive people and subordinates respond to that attraction. Above all, for the many people who have few or no leadership skills, influencing the leader is the next best thing.

All this flattery, lying and general admiration can prove highly dysfunctional to the judgement skills of the leader. Eventually they begin to think they are always right. People start to give them the answers they want rather than the data they need. Then they take wrong decisions. After a long enough period, the leader loses the independent-minded, better quality employees and gets surrounded by increasingly mediocre people. Eventually, the leader loses touch with reality. One sure indicator that this has happened is that they begin to believe they are worth a much greater salary and rewards package, in the very year when they deliver terrible results. They may become infected with 'chairmanitis' – (a condition wherein they need everybody to address them by their title rather than by their first name, which was good enough for the first 30 years of their career. Eventually the leader loses the job. It comes as a total surprise!

Lessons for leaders

Is there a key lesson in all the above? First, I cannot emphasize enough how important it is for leaders to know themselves better than anybody around them. If they know their own weaknesses, these can be turned to strengths, because they can gather people who compensate for their own shortcomings and balance their personal power. It is useful to use any tools that are available for analysis of both oneself and one's subordinates. This will indicate where the greatest efforts need to be made to achieve increasing mastery of self and understanding of others. Aggregation of team results can give insights into the culture and climate of the organization. A leader should know what their preferred style of leadership is and try to adjust it in the light of the situations the organization passes through. If they realize they do not have and cannot successfully transform into the style that is necessary for a crisis or a change in the fortunes of the organization, then it is always wiser to jump before being pushed. Either that, or find a transitional leader to achieve the necessary changes.

Finally, leaders should always be aware of the power that emanates from the leadership position, and understand how it attracts flatterers and sycophants. Do not be seduced. Learn to use the power wisely. It is easy to be a big personality from the leadership position. Do not become seduced by the nonsense which can so easily attach itself to leaders. Be careful – today's halo is tomorrow's noose!

RECOMMENDED READING FOR CHAPTER 4

Belbin, R. M. (1991) *Management Teams*. Oxford: Butterworth Heinemann.

Belbin, M. (1993) *Team Roles at Work*. Oxford: Butterworth Heinemann.

Briggs-Myers, I. (1992) *Gifts Differing*. Palo Alto, CA.: Consulting Psychologists Press.

Chapman, E. N. (1977) *Your Attitude is Showing*. Palo Alto, CA: Science Research Associates.

Ferrucci, P. (1990) *What We May Be*. London: Aquarian/Thorsons.

Goleman, D. (1996) *Emotional Intelligence*. London: Bloomsbury.

Kiersey, D. and Bates, M. (1984) *Please Understand Me*. Del Mar, CA: Prometheus Nemesis Book Company.

Lewis, R. and Lowe, P. (1992) *Individual Excellence*. London: Kogan Page.

Schultz, C. (1955) *FIRO: A three-dimensional theory of interpersonal behaviour*. New York: Holt, Rinehart and Winston.

Biographies of companies and leaders

Bayer, T. (1991) *Maxwell: The Outsider*. London: Mandarin.

Colier, P. and Horowitz, D. (1976) *The Rockefellers*. New York: Signet.

Davies, H. (1981) *The Grades*. London: Weidenfeld & Nicolson.

Gittin N. and Masters, K. (1997) *Hit and Run*. New York: Simon & Schuster.

Heller, R. (1993) *The Super Chiefs*. New York: Truman Talley/Plume.

Love, J. F. (1995) *McDonald's: Behind the Arches*. New York: Bantam.

Malik, R. (1975) *And Tomorrow the World?* London: Millington.

Maney, K. (1995) *Megamedia Shakeout*. New York: John Wiley.

Morita, A. (1994) *Made in Japan*. London: HarperCollins.

Shawcross, W. (1992) *Murdoch*. London: Chatto & Windus.

Walton, S. (1993) *Made in America*. New York: Bantam.

Wanstell, G. (1987) *Tycoon*. London: Grafton.

LEADERSHIP, DECISIONS AND BUSINESS SUCCESS

....

This chapter defines the differences between decision making for leaders and other types of manager. It defines different ways of approaching strategic decisions. I emphasize that leaders should remain primarily involved in strategic, rather than ordinary, decisions. People managing a total career should always take their decisions with the whole perspective in mind.

....

Case study 5.1

YOU CAN NEVER TAKE TOO *FEW* DECISIONS

Great leaders take few decisions because they realize that any leader's decisions they take can cause great disruption to their organization. They therefore aim to take few but excellent decisions. For example, the managing director of a large transport supply business in the UK, was said to have taken only two key decisions in five years as leader. The first was to reduce the number of regional divisions from seven to five. This enabled him to remove two less than adequate leaders without singling them out for punishment. It also sent a warning signal to the five surviving managing directors. They subsequently worked ferociously hard during that leader's remaining years, in case he again decided to reduce the number of regions. The only other decision he took was *not* to take any more decisions. In retrospect, those were the best years ever in the history of that business.

STRATEGIC DECISIONS

Strategic decisions for leaders, are defined as those which may affect the long-term health and prosperity of the organization. The opening case study illustrates that, by and large, it is probably a wise counsel for leaders to stick to the large strategic decisions, whenever they can. These will usually involve the following topics:

- long-term product and market development
- the development of human resources for the organization
- movement from mature industrial sectors into developing industries
- expansion into new growth sectors
- closure of mature, undesirable market interests
- changes of corporate culture to adapt and prepare for the future
- major additions to the core competencies* of the organization.

* Core competencies are the most important aspects of 'know how' within any business. They are the skills, knowledge and techniques that form its competitive edge and ability to make profits (*see* Hamel and Pralahad 1994).

The reason for advocating fewer but better decisions is that when leaders get involved with the minutiae of detail of their organizations, they can do considerable harm. This is not to say that leaders should not know about such detail. Nor that they should not take detail into account when taking decisions. Rather, it is suggested that they should not take decisions on small and unimportant matters. It distracts them from the major and important factors. It also diminishes the skills of their subordinates, since every time leaders take decisions that are really the province of a subordinate person in the organization, they deprive that person of a learning opportunity. There is also a greater chance of the boss making the wrong decision than the subordinate. The leader probably knows less about the detail of the problem and brings less expertise and knowledge to the decision than the subordinate.

> **When leaders get involved with the minutiae of detail of their organizations, they can do considerable harm.**

Short-term decisions with long-term consequences

Many apparently short-term, decisions can have much longer-term potential consequences. The leader's expertise should be to know which they are and focus on the ones with the most profound strategic long-term effects. For example, all culture change decisions are likely to have long-term effects. They can cause profound corporate scar tissue. So although decisions to change the culture ('the way we do things around here') can be taken easily and look like a one- or two-year process, it is rare that the culture can be changed, in medium and large organizations, in less than five to ten years. Sometimes there may not be enough time to change the culture before the organization dies.

Sometimes an organization gets into a rapidly accelerating spiral of decay. There are multiple types of strategic causes of this situation. A list of examples could contain the following:

- the permanent loss of market share
- the growth of rival firms who compete more successfully
- the growth of bad habits within the business
- sudden discovery of accumulated mistakes in the accounting process

- technological disadvantage from rival businesses' R&D breakthroughs
- the sudden death of a great leader in the early stages of leadership (later a competent leader would have a successor in place)
- a one-off catastrophe such as product failure. For example: contamination was found in some bottles of Perrier water. The slow reaction of the leadership team had a catastrophic effect on the long-term confidence of consumers in the product. This example can be compared with the exemplary and swift reaction of the leadership of the pharmaceutical company producing the pain killer Tylenol. When somebody deliberately poisoned a few packs in a blackmail threat they withdrew and destroyed all stocks of Tylenol from shop shelves. When the pain killer was put back on the shelves it was welcomed back to triumphant acclaim. The visible sign how much the company cared was symbolized in the new tamper-proof packaging. By contrast, Perrier came back onto the supermarket shelves with no symbolism showing that the accident could never happen again. It never recovered its market share.

It could be argued that several of the situations listed above should never have reached catastrophic levels because a good leader would have perceived the first signs and reacted to them long before the crisis. But that would imply an organization in a state of continuous perfection and few manage that. It is also worth noting that it is only under the extreme circumstances listed above, that drastic *cultural* action is recommended. Similarly, it must usually be considered foolhardy to risk 'killing the patient completely, by removing limbs, to save the body of the business. Incidentally, many of the radical downsizing operations of the workforce, that a multitude of businesses undertook throughout the 1980s and early 1990s, were akin this sort of major surgery.

Decisions about product and service quality are usually strategically important. For example, at L'Oréal, one of the world's leading beauty products manufacturers, a decision to change a single line of the hair style on the picture of the model on their Elnett Hair lacquer (a world leading brand), goes to the main board in Paris for approval. L'Oréal has become one of the leading suppliers of hair and body preparations in the world. They maintain their position by being obsessively focused about the detail of their key products and brands.

Drastic changes in human resource policies can reverberate for decades. In the early 1980s, when John Harvey-Jones was in the chair at ICI, he decided to change the ICI human resource policy of 'jobs for life'. He wanted to declare the first £1 billion profit year in the history of the business. He achieved that goal, in part, by making thousands of people redundant. This was the first time ever in the history of ICI that such a level of profit had been reached. One cannot judge, even now, whether it was right to change the guarantee that ICI offered of 'a job for life'. There should be no doubt, however, that the amazing loyalty and dedication to ICI that the workers had felt before he took that action, was changed for ever.

Decisions to change the structural design of an organization are always complex and difficult. For a start, the structure of the business is the main guide to everybody within the organization as to how the business works. It organizes people into appropriate work units. It describes the promotion system and where the next job prospects within the organization might lie. It also states levels of authority and who is in charge of whom. It delineates where the power lies and who may use it upon whom. Thus, structure is a sensitive matter. When leaders decide to change the structural design of a business, they should first prepare their planned changes in private discussions with their human resources adviser, and then *implement the changes quickly*. Structural change always induces massive insecurity before, during, and after the event. People behave more politically and dress up their results to ensure their place in the new structure. They take their eyes off any budgetary or other motivational objectives they may have had before any announcements about the structure change. I always recommend to leaders that they should take all structure change decisions themselves, with the assistance, perhaps, of a human resources expert. That should at least ensure minimum disruption. If the new structure involves losing people as well, it is wise to never drag out the process, but to do it humanely and with the minimum damage to people (it always looks bad afterwards). If personnel remain in their posts during long periods of notice, they can ruin morale. Remember that it is as important for the business to look after the survivors as those who leave. There is evidence that shows that those who depart tend to get on with the rest of their lives. But the evidence also shows that those who stay remain fearful, uncertain and untrusting. For a long time afterwards they believe that the sword might still fall upon them and they are often more demotivated than those who have been made redundant.

Long-term decisions with strategic import

These involve anything to do with new markets, international expansion, developing new skills and core competencies or investing a large percentage of the organization's capital resources (therefore locking up the firm's wealth flow for many years). In fact, anything that the analysts, Wall Street, the London Stock Exchange, stock-brokers and investors regard as changing the nature of the company should be considered a long-term decision with strategic import. These are the really substantive decisions of which the average leader will take only five or six in his whole career. If he takes more than this it will be either because he is running a global corporation with divisions around the world, or because he is taking too many decisions! Such decisions require much preparation and careful thought. They require the input of multiple sources of data. They are also typical of the kind of decision the success of which may be impossible to judge until many years after the leader has drawn his final success bonus and departed.

Decisions to exit key markets or areas of interest are also difficult because they frequently involve writing off large amounts of corporate assets. One may not be aware until it is too late that such decisions also carry the danger of destroying corporate wealth.

The opportunities for writing off large amounts of corporate assets only occur when leaders decide to do big things such as enter major new industries or exit apparently mature ones. Changes of key personnel, such as board members or the leaders of important divisions of a corporation, often have long-term effects, even though it does not feel like it at the time.

There are many positive examples. Bob Bauman was the leader of SmithKline Beecham (SB). He did an outstanding job combining Smith Kline and French with a long-established pharmaceutical firm, Beechams. I participated in developing some of the programmes to effect the merger between SmithKline and Beecham. It rarely felt as if it was being successfully achieved, because there was much angst among the managers of the business, worrying whether they would survive the merger process. But it was successfully completed, largely through the determination of Bob Bauman to achieve a culture that encapsulated the best of the cultures and work habits of both the merging firms. Another leader in a similar mould is Sir Richard Sykes. He is the executive chairman of Glaxo Wellcome, although the 'Wellcome' part was a consequence of a brilliant takeover he led, making the business one of the leading pharmaceutical organizations in the world. The leadership wisdom and empathy that goes into successfully merging two large businesses, composed largely of bright, scientifically qualified, highly trained personnel, is of a high order. Most mergers fail. When they succeed, it is highly laudable and evidence of great leadership.

OPTIMAL AND SUB-OPTIMAL DECISION MAKING

The concept of decision making belongs more in the realm of economics rather than that of leadership, because defining decisions in terms of optimal and sub-optimal is equivalent to judging a decision through the standards of a time-horizon judgement machine. Today's sub-optimal choice may be tomorrow's brilliant investment decision. Vickers, the engineering business which also owns Rolls-Royce cars,

> Today's sub-optimal choice may be tomorrow's brilliant investment decision.

has (1998) put the car business up for sale. It looks like a crazy decision to sell off, for a few hundred million £s, one of the world's most eminent car brand names. Have the leaders who took that decision done their homework? Perhaps background analysis has demonstrated to the Vickers' leaders that all prestige car manufacture is going to hit the buffers and this is

> History is always written by the victors.

an optimum time to sell out. That would make the decision to sell look like optimal decision making by geniuses. However, one suspects that it is more likely to turn out to be a sub-optimal decision by nominal leaders. The purchaser will find the Rolls-Royce brand name to be a money spinner for many decades. The decision makers at Vickers will continue to collect their pensions long after the sub-optimality of their leadership decisions has been revealed in its appropriate light!

Of course sub-optimality may be more appearance than reality. History is always written by the victors. If a leader fails to sell a decision to the board, if they are subsequently dismissed, their decision will be described as 'awful' by their successors. It is incumbent upon leaders to ensure that decisions are widely accepted as the best possible, given all the circumstances. To do that, the leader has to stay in place to defend the decision. Many readers will know the old leadership joke about the outgoing boss who leaves three envelopes in his desk as a guide for the new incumbent of the desk. Envelope number one contains the advice, 'blame everything that goes wrong in the first year upon your predecessor'. A year goes by and business is not good. So he opens the second envelope. It says: 'restructure the company'. He follows this advice and attributes the following year's bad results to the costs of restructuring. But matters don't improve. So he opens the third envelope. It reads: 'prepare three envelopes …'.

One question, which may be used to judge whether a particular decision is optimal, is to ask whether it opens new strategic horizons which were not available previously. At the end of the day, the best insurance against poor leaders taking sub-optimal decisions is the excellence of the board of directors. It is the role of a quality board to recognize sub-optimality early and not be afraid to act on their findings, even if it means throwing the culprit out. Optimal decisions deliver the best possible result over the longest feasible term that the organization should contemplate, given its size and ambitions.

It is *never* acceptable to take sub-optimal decisions if you know that's what they are at the time. The difficulty is knowing, in advance, what is sub-optimal. Unfortunately, only time can prove a decision to have been unwise. But how can one judge the quality of a decision in the short term? One has to use different criteria:

- intuition (or the sheer obvious *post hoc* intelligence or stupidity of the decision)
- the judgement of peer groups (the board, investors, etc.)
- ask the leader to explain.

Let's examine each in turn.

Intuition

Intuition is a highly underrated source of insight. In its style, it can be similar to that special quality children have, when they make direct, and incisive observations that cut to the heart of events they observe. We often ascribe this capacity of children to be direct to their having less consciousness cluttering their mind. If that is true, perhaps leaders need to take a leaf from their book. When confronted with a dilemma, good leaders often have intuitive, immediate reactions which indicate the best response to it. It is only after they start to examine the arguments for and against their first idea that they lose touch with their original intuition.

Case study 5.2

FOLLOW YOUR INTUITION

I was advising the leader of an entertainment business which occupied the number two position in its industry. He received a cheeky takeover proposal from the leader of the business in the number five position in the industry. Intuition said, 'this is a rotten idea – let's reject immediately'. But caution, and the modern fear of legal action by shareholders, made him consider the offer. The leader of the other business was smooth and skilled at the arts of persuasion. He was almost convinced by him. These talks went on for six months. Of course, they leaked to the market. The morale of people in his organization began to sag. Eventually he was reminded of his original instincts. He 'helicoptered' above the debate and saw that rejection of the bid was a 'no-brainer'. He threw out the proposal the next day. Not, however, before it had done real harm to his business. It had always been a bad idea that a company with one-third the capital of his business, one-third the number of customers, a rotten infrastructure and a bad market situation could contemplate taking over his corporation. However, as he had started to analyze the situation and allow the other, sweet-talking leader to begin to exploit his powers of persuasion, he had become hypnotized for a short time. If he had gone with his original intuition he would have been saved a lot of agony and trouble for his employees and himself.

Intuition often works by drawing the observer's notice to the obvious. Consider the example of the building of the Channel Tunnel as a commercial venture. Although it is an admirable achievement to have built it at all, it was always destined to be an all-time great business blunder. It never had commercial viability. Reflect on the behaviour of British Gas, which used to have a monopoly on gas supply in the UK. Their leadership practically declared war on the industry regulator. The concept of a powerful monopoly attacking its regulator was self-evidently misguided. It will be seen as one of the sillier industrial actions of late-20th century industry in the UK. Subsequently, British Gas then rewarded the CEO and the chairman for the insightfulness of their leadership decisions with retirement packages of internationally generous dimensions.

The judgement of peer groups (the board, investors, etc.)

When it comes to judging the quality of decisions, there are peer groups who are properly qualified. A well-constituted board of directors should be a residual body of collective wisdom. Unfortunately, in the UK even the best boards rarely work up the power or aggression to do anything useful before it is too late. Although, individually, they often recognize stupidity, they see themselves powerless to act as a group until the situation is so acute that they can do little to help. I discuss elsewhere in this book why any quality leader should be able to deliver improved results within a year of taking office, because there are always methods to make this happen. If a leader doesn't know the short-term tricks of profit-making, there is little reason to assume he understands properly the skills of long-term strategic investment.

Compare those examples with the fact that the leaders of Britain's premier businesses regularly vote on who they consider to be the best business leader among their peer group. They regularly vote for people such as Sir Richard Greenbury, the leader of Marks & Spencer, rapidly becoming a leading international retailer of clothing and food. They have also approved Jan Leschley, the leader who has taken SmithKline Beecham from the bottom of the world's top ten pharmaceuticals to among the world leaders.

Ask the leader to explain

It is astonishing how poorly most leaders and their key stakeholders communicate with each other. One frequently finds that an inordinate amount of time is spent speculating as to whether the CEO's latest decision is intelligent. All too often, colleagues and subordinates fail to ask the leader to explain a decision. They could ask, quite simply, 'What factors did you take into account when you decided this? Were you aware of all these other variables that we think are relevant and important?' I have often wondered why they don't! There are some valid reasons. Sometimes they feel that if they ask and then don't like the answers, they might be obliged to do something about it – even take action which might be premature. At other times, it could be because they are afraid that they will look stupid for asking, because the answers might be so obvious that they will feel that they should have known without being told. This fear of looking stupid accounts for a lot of the behaviour in corporate board rooms. Readers may wish to furnish their own explanations for this.

Fear of looking stupid accounts for a lot of the behaviour in corporate board rooms. Readers may wish to furnish their own explanations for this.

TAKING DECISIONS WHEN THERE ARE 'BLACK HOLES' IN THE DATA

Sometimes a decision may look sub-optimal because some of the components of the decision include unknowable factors, or data which has to be guessed at. Poor quality leaders may be aware of what data is missing and become highly stressed about taking any decision at all. They will usually postpone the decision until it becomes either irrelevant or too late.

By comparison, one of the most marked aspects of some of the great leaders I have met, is their ability to take decisions in spite of there being vast quantities of apparently relevant and important data missing from the file. Gifted leaders, who have superior judgement, can somehow fill in the missing data points and take the decision anyway. This can be observed time and again. They do not actually guess the data. However, they seem to make prognostications which arrive at a decision which will work strategically. They can do this no matter what form the data eventually arrives in. It is an uncanny ability and, for me, it is the ultimate proof that I am working with a great leader. I don't encounter it often. Consider the following example:

Case study 5.3

BLACK PAINT HOLES

In the days when ICI was chaired by Sir John Harvey-Jones, one of ICI's larger businesses was the manufacture of paint, mainly for industrial use. The paints division was led in those days by Ronnie (later Sir Ronnie) Hampel who also subsequently, became Chairman of ICI. Sir John and the ICI Board did not want to take the decision to step up from being an important UK and European paints manufacturer to becoming a global player in the paint industry. At that time they had too many other, more pressing investment priorities. However, they did not want to lose the opportunity to decide to be a global player if later data and analysis indicated that this would be wise. This meant allowing a takeover opportunity for acquiring a big paints manufacturer which dominated the USA to pass them by and go to another owner. The American company was too big and buying it would have committed ICI to be a global player because of the sheer size of the business resulting from such a takeover. Simultaneously, however, there was a much smaller French firm available which had received a bid from a competitor of ICI. If the French business went to the competition, that could lock ICI out of the European paint trade forever. Furthermore, if ICI were to step in and buy the French business they could do so without being committed to the global strategy. So they bought the French paint company but let the US opportunity go past. Ronnie Hampel also argued, at that time, that the French company, which was in private hands, might never come back onto the market but the US company would probably remain in play because it was quoted on the NY Stock Exchange. Fifteen years later, ICI bought the US business and completed its positioning to be a global player in the world paint industry!

BALANCING THE STAKEHOLDERS

Balancing the interests of all the stakeholders is a special art that all great leaders must acquire because there is almost never a situation where there are no contradictory stakeholder interests.

Herbert Simon, an economics Nobel Prize winning academic, developed a theory that all decision making in business organizations had to be sub-optimal decisions by definition; all leaders have to take decisions which take account of many different groups' interests. Those groups have contradictory objectives. The leader always has to balance the interests and power of the stakeholders within the business. Simon called this phenomenon *satisficing*. Balancing the interests of all the stakeholders is a special art that all great leaders must acquire because there is almost never a situation where there are no contradictory stakeholder interests. It can be the most satisfying aspect of a leader's work and should not be underestimated.

The organizational stakeholders range from banks and other financial institutions, to shareholders, debenture holders, stock holders, trade unions, staff and other employees, customers and suppliers. In short, every group of people who need to be taken into account when deciding what to do with the organization, when to do it, and how much to achieve (in profits, investment, number of employees, quantity of buildings, land, other assets, etc.)

Consider Figure 5.1 below, showing a list of stakeholders. Think about who you consider to be the most, and who the least, important, with regard to an assessment of profitability within a business.

If we examine the fairly simplistic assessments in the Figure, both customers and workers might want less profit; customers, because they would consider more profit means higher prices for the products or services; workers, because higher profits mean less money available for wages. It is astonishing how often one hears company spokespersons delivering nonsense such as, 'everybody wants our business to be healthy and have large profits which demonstrate that health!' They even do it on a communications medium being viewed by either their customers or workers and they thus alienate members of their key stakeholder constituencies. Some

Fig. 5.1 STAKEHOLDERS AND THEIR ATTITUDES TOWARDS PROFITABILITY

Business stakeholder theory, conceived by the Nobel Prize winner Professor Herbert Simon, states that a leader always has to take essentially sub-optimal decisions, because the many stakeholders in a business have contradictory preferred outcomes from the results of the organization's activities. In the figure, a set of typical stakeholders is differentiated on the single criterion of who prefers more, and who less, profit to be made by the business.

leaders make the same mistake. All the other stakeholders in the Figure want greater profits – but for different reasons. For example, owners want them if they are shareholders, because profits should lead to increased dividends. Lenders want increased profits in order to decrease the risks inherent in the loans they have made to the business, hopefully without a corresponding decrease in the interest rate they charge (which is how they increase their own profits).

The key theme of stakeholder theory is that the stakeholders often have conflicting requirements from a business, on much more complex issues than profitability. For example, although the employees want the highest possible levels of remuneration, and the shareholders might want lower levels of wages to ensure higher profits and dividends, the different lenders might want completely different approaches. Debenture holders (fully secured lenders) might not want the business to be launching too many new products because these are risky and endanger the safe income of the debenture holders. Ordinary shareholders want those product launches because any one great new product adopted by the customers might increase the share price multi-fold. On the other hand, the bankers may prefer a low-risk approach. Senior managers of the corporation, who may be on high levels of bonus for short-term achievement, might want to take greater risks to achieve their objectives and bonuses earlier. Should the firm pay higher dividends to underpin the share price or higher wages to attract the best employees? If managers believe that raw materials supply is a key to the future of their industry, they might negotiate with suppliers in a conciliatory manner. However, if they pay higher prices to suppliers, should they then keep wages to workers low or product prices high or merely moderate dividends to shareholders?

Stakeholder theory demonstrates that managers and leaders are always making trade-offs between conflicting demands as to how resources should be allocated. This requires fine judgement which, ultimately, is what they are paid for. It indicates another area where a leader requires absolute balance and precise judgement skills in an objective equilibrium condition. They need to juggle more complex elements than any computer could calculate. Again, this points to the importance of the need for a leader to have a finely balanced emotional condition, both as stable background and for equilibrium when assessing and taking such decisions. It also demonstrates the ultimate leadership decision making qualities have to be perspective and judgement. When these are aligned with the determination to render decisions successful, it is an unbeatable combination.

TREATING THE ORGANIZATION AS A SOCIAL ENTITY

Arie de Geus, formerly at Shell Petroleum and currently an academic at the London Business School has examined many of the longest surviving economic organizations. His general findings are that the key explanatory variables for organizational longevity is their employment of social and ethical objectives in addition to business aims, as a measure of success. They also seem to have a capacity for reinventing themselves in new forms, by moving from one industrial sector to another as various markets start up, grow, mature, and then die. The businesses which survive the longest do not appear to focus too much on maximizing profits but they do focus on optimizing profits. This means that their leaders, over the very long run, take a rational view about how much they need to make to satisfy their owners, compared to how much they need to invest to look after the other stakeholders, such as the staff (who need income, dependable jobs and continuity of employment). Another variable that is common in many long-lived businesses is continuity of ownership, or influence by the same family over long periods of time. It appears to be easier for families to pass on a deep-rooted value system than corporate leaders. A UK example is the John Lewis Partnership, which distributes most of its profits in annual bonuses to the staff. The leader treats the business as a trust, to provide income and job satisfaction (among other objectives), which he helps to deliver on behalf of the staff first of all, and then the customers.

These findings form a most powerful argument for any leader who is asked to justify treating a business organization as much as a social entity as a profit-maximizing apparatus. This can be most important when the shareholders are emphasizing their legal rights to demand that the leader exploit the organization's resources to maximize returns for themselves. The leader should ask over what period they wish him to consider the maximization of their investment. The longer they want the organization to exist the greater should be the treatment of it as a social entity. That will maximize loyalty and longevity. De Geus's work demonstrates that even within profit-making business organizations social values can be superior to purely economic ones. The leader still has to decide what the bulk of the organization's particular stakeholders will accept and prefer. Interestingly, another new science, sociobiology, would probably define long-term decisions as being the best and most genetically intelligent. After all, children inherit shares when organizations survive and sociobiology would define children as the best form of genetic longevity. It also happens to be *the way of the heart*. Many suspect that it is superior to the way of the mind alone.

GETTING THE RIGHT INPUTS TO DECISIONS

The key factors in decision making are:

- time
- timing
- quantity of resources
- number of employees
- capacity to take complex decisions
- capacity to explain and communicate decisions
- capacity of the organization to implement the decision
- need to improve skills and core competencies of the organization.

Let's consider each in turn.

Time

Leaders need a keen sense of time – past, present and future. They need to take account of what the organization has done, when it did it, and how. The leader needs to know how, in the past, the organization changed its own condition or its market interests, in order to understand better what to do in the future. This sense of time must also be aligned with their personal situation, not necessarily selfishly but with relevance. For example, how much longer do they intend to work within the organization? Will they be able to see through the consequences of their decisions and, if not, are they about to take the type of decision where they can ensure that a successor will understand it sufficiently well, and believe in it enough, to sustain it and bring it to fruition?

Timing

Bringing any decision to fruition requires a very fine sense of timing. Is it the right time for the relevant stakeholders? Is the board ready for this particular key decision? If not now, when will the timing be right? These are the key elements of leadership decision making. Great leaders do it instinctively. But those who agonize about it should note that most leaders find timing the most difficult element of the decision-making process. My observations over many years lead me to believe that hesitancy nearly always works out to be the best policy. If you are still asking yourself questions about whether the timing is right, it is probably your intuition that is telling you that the timing is premature. The one exception to deliberate and careful use of hesitancy is when many members of the organization are expecting a change of structure. Restructuring an organization can be highly destabilizing for the people who work for the business, at any level, as well as for the customers. In these cases, my earlier advice to do it fast and get it over still applies. With that proviso, however, reflect on the following case study, which amply illustrates the value of deliberately waiting for the right moment.

> My observations over many years lead me to believe that hesitancy nearly always works out to be the best policy. If you are still asking yourself questions about whether the timing is right, it is probably your intuition that is telling you that the timing is premature.

Case study 5.4

BIDING HIS TIME ...

A leader in the telecommunications industry appeared to be faced with a *fait accompli* by a fellow shareholder who owned 25 per cent of the stock of a large business which, in earlier times, had a valuation of £2bn. Over a couple of years the value had decreased and it was presently valued at about £800m. The other shareholder (whose parent corporation was in cash-flow difficulties) wanted to sell his share of the business to a third party, for what looked like too low a price. My client, who tended to take a longer-term point of view, believed that the price the fellow shareholder wanted to accept did not take sufficient account of the underlying value of the business. In addition, he did not like the fact that his equal major-

▶

ity controlling rights might be eroded or lost to another business leader he didn't know or trust. So he bided his time ...

He also investigated the bidding company and discovered they were not running their business as well as his managers were running his and their own. He also knew that his partner was short of cash and cash flow. So he bided his time ...

Eventually his partner tried to force his hand by bringing in lawyers to threaten him with a lawsuit if he continued to block the bid for his block of shares. But my client pointed out that their agreement meant that they had to give each other a first option to buy each other's shares at the same price that any third party offered to pay. He would be willing to do so. And he bided his time ...

He offered to buy out his partner. The partner began to ask himself why his partner would want to keep the business so much, even increase his stake. The partner wanted cash *today* from the external buyer, but my client insisted on his rights. And he bided his time ...

Meanwhile, they had a chance to buy another business and win a leading position in the industry in that country. The potential bidder disappeared from the scene. But he bided his time ...

Eventually he persuaded the board to make the bid; the partner jumped at the opportunity to join in. The wise leader stopped biding his time ...

Biding one's time can often be the best way to get to an optimal decision!

Quantity of resources

In the business world of the late 20th century, the quantity of financial resources should never be a problem. The world abounds with vast and varied ready sources of capital and equity. There is never a shortage of money. Rather there is a profound shortage of good ideas. If any business has insufficient resources it can easily find them. On occasions, when it can't, it is usually for excellent reasons. If a bank won't lend to them, it's because the risks are probably too great for an ordinary banker's risk-averse attitudes; why not persuade the shareholders to put in more equity? If they don't want to, is that because they are not pleased with what you have been doing with their equity so far? What about trying a high-interest junk bonds issue? If the junk bond dealers don't want to touch it, is that because you or your organization have let them down previously, on other matters? If not, is it because they consider this particular idea a non-runner? It could be that it's the leader whom they distrust. If it's the idea they don't like, give up the idea. If it's the leader, perhaps he or she should consider resignation, for the sake of the idea and the organization?

The number of employees

When we considered the factors necessary to achieve longevity in an organization, consideration of the people it employed was seen to be paramount. These concepts would lead one to take great care when decreasing the number of employees. The number of employees within a business should be a direct function of need, history and organizational slack (the amount of spare resources around the business). Drastic haste, whether in increasing or decreasing the number of people employed, is always dangerous. The former, because rapid increases mean that there is insufficient time to ensure that recruits are properly inducted to take on the organization's values; the latter, because once you have broken faith with your employees with large-scale redundancy programmes, like a broken piece of china the organization will never be quite the same again.

Capacity to take complex decisions

This may refer to both the leader and the organization. The leader's capacity to take complex decisions is merely a function of intelligence. If they cannot do it, they probably won't be bright enough to realize they are actually facing a complex decision. But one must also ask whether the organization can deal with a complex decision? I wrote earlier (in Chapter Two) about my research findings on time horizons. Are there enough people at the top of the firm, with sufficiently long time horizons, to understand the complex decision and translate it into simple enough messages for the rest of the business to understand and operationalize? Will the people in operations, marketing and sales find a way to explain it to their relevant groups of people? Can the decision be sold to the City or to Wall Street?

For example, one of my clients, a UK-quoted corporation, had recently developed a poor performance record with the City analysts and stock brokers. Consequently its shares were poorly valued and its leadership was held in low esteem. Even when it successfully changed its cost structure by maintaining its performance while reducing its employed workforce by 25 per cent (from 6000 to 4500) and its annual costs by 10 per cent, it still failed to convince the City it had great leadership and had turned the corner. It had taken complex decisions, implemented them successfully in a very short term (six months). The only way it could finally change the attitudes of the important influencers who could affect how it was perceived by investors, was to invest in a massive PR exercise to change their minds, both about the business and its leadership.

Capacity to explain and communicate decisions

The capacity to explain and communicate a decision is a direct consequence of the previous subject. Complex decisions take a lot of explaining. It is probably necessary to devise a completely separate communications strategy to ensure that a particularly important decision will be fully understood both within and without the organization. It should never be assumed that people will accept a decision without explanation. That does not mean they need, or will be able to understand the total complexity of the decision. The leader will have to judge how to communicate the decision with a clear story line, which remains thoroughly honest, while still explaining enough to convince people that it is a relevant and optimal solution.

Capability of the organization to implement decisions

Another fine judgement skill when making decisions, is deciding whether the organization has the capability to successfully implement a great idea. Good strategic ideas are a common enough currency. Most organizations have great ideas floating around. Often people with great ideas think they alone are bright enough to have had the idea and everybody else in the business is essentially uninspired. Not so. Great ideas are common currency. The power and skill to implement them is the rare currency. Knowing when an idea is implementable is the key question to be assessed by the leader. They must know what they must do to make the organization more fit to eventually take that decision in the future, if the organization is currently short of the necessary capability or core competencies. I was present at a classic

> **Great ideas are common currency. The power and skill to implement them is the rare currency.**

example of a situation such as this in the directors' dining room at a major business. This particular organization is immensely rich, although not necessarily successful in industry. The top executive I was with was speculating about all the exciting takeovers he could make with all his reserves of capital. In particular, he speculated that he might decide to take over a large UK business, to rocket his business to the top echelons of the global industry. One week later, the business he was coveting announced a proposed merger with a competitor, forming a combined operation which would become the leading business in the world in its field. In years past this business had been beaten at the post by one of these rivals for another takeover opportunity. Evidently its capacity to implement great ideas, as compared to their capacity to conceive them, had not improved.

The need to improve the skills and core competencies of the organization

Leaders should be continuously reviewing the state of the organization and taking decisions on how to improve its core competencies and skills. Getting the organization more ready for future problems and opportunities than it has been in the past is a prime responsibility of leadership. Such decisions are being taken all the time, by default if not deliberately. Examples here would be: the type of people who are being recruited to the organization; the amount of investment in the business's equipment and IT; the training that is creating current attitudes and cultures prevailing in the business; and the receptiveness of the most important stakeholders to change when it is necessary.

Guarantees of optimal outcomes from decisions

For the leader it is not difficult. Great leaders know they have optimized. The rest is just a measure of their determination to deliver all the predicted outcomes, no matter what external events arise which could not have been predicted at the time of the actual decision. This capacity determinedly to carry a decision through to a successful implementation is one of the strongest facets of great leaders. To a certain extent, it almost begs the question of whether a decision can be optimal. A decision will be optimal when a good leader takes it and is determined to ensure it happens.

What about the other interested parties? They may need to be convinced of both the previous and current correctness of the decision. They have to be taught to trust their decision takers. However, they, too, must use their intuition to inform them whether a decision is turning out as predicted. Are the defined measures to test the correctness of the decision meeting the predicted outcomes? Are there sufficient, fundamental litmus tests* to measure success along the critical path of the implementation process?

THE HELICOPTER TOOL

I developed a useful mental tool which others tend to refer to as 'helicoptering' above problems. What does it mean? It is a device to get things into perspective. Earlier in this book, I covered concepts relating to emotional maturity and their importance relative to pure intelligence. Helicoptering is one of the ways one can learn to use emotional maturity and perspective to avoid over- or under-reacting to events, especially those where one's emotions of fear or anger are aroused and one is in danger of reacting wrongly, emotionally, in the heat of the moment.

The best helicoptering method I have developed, is to place everything into a time horizon machine. How do you use your time machine? First, whenever some catastrophe or apparent disaster befalls you, you must ask yourself, 'how important will it be in, possibly, three months time?' If it still feels it will be relevant and still hurt, ask yourself, again, 'how impor-

* See p. 151.

tant will it be in one year's time?' If that still feels painful, try to put it into a three-year time horizon. Will you even remember the incident without looking it up in your diary? If it still feels painful in the three-year time machine test, try ten years. It is astonishing how few incidents or events really rate as important, in the ten-year perspective. If it still ranks high when placed in a ten-year perspective, I suggest you become seriously anxious. You are going to need all the adrenaline you can muster!

THE 'LITMUS TEST' CONCEPT

Many leaders use some form of the concept of what I would describe as a 'litmus test'. In chemistry, litmus paper is used to indicate clearly, by turning red or blue, whether a substance is acidic or alkaline. Litmus tests by leaders are rarely so clear-cut. However, they do have to theorize about everything around them. This includes people and their personal development potential, future events, outcomes from strategic decisions or expected results from installations of new technology. Their litmus tests do not usually give such clear indications as the chemical ones. But they still give excellent signals to the competent leader, who may set both small and large tests, create both low and high hurdles for their managers, and set deadlines or budgets which test the full range of the limits of the managers they expect to follow in their footsteps. When their people give appropriate indications on these litmus tests, sensible leaders move the hurdles, to test them further. If somebody fails them, the leader will draw the necessary conclusions. That will not mean that the person is either unworthy or a failure, but that the last barrier, the one they failed to surmount, marks the limit of their subordinate's current capacity and skills as a leader. That is what a quality litmus test does.

For example, one leader I used to work with had almost no strategic skills, although he was astonishingly inspired in using people strategically. He did this by setting litmus tests about their personal development, with a rough timetable in his own mind predicting when they would reach particular peaks. When his people achieved those skill levels (he never told them his expectations – that's how he kept the litmus test valid) he would promote them and make his next prediction. Although this leader was useless at strategy, he was so good at exploiting clever subordinates and maximizing the use of their strategic skills that he had a successful career up to a level of £80 million revenue business.

Such predictions about the development of the capacities and skills of the people surrounding the leader in the organization also help develop the quality of the leader's own judgement. They use litmus tests to assess their own progress, too. It should be noted that wise leaders use their predictions about the future of individuals and events, not only to find successors and promotees but also to freeze somebody at their discovered level of competence. Much more damage is done to individuals when they are promoted above their skill capacity than is ever done by not promoting them early enough.

It is worth noting some special conditions about the use of litmus tests, if one is going to employ them successfully. First, when setting imagined targets of behaviour for people and waiting for them to fulfil the predictions, it is important not to tell the person concerned of the expectations for them. That would distort the power of the litmus test method. You could never evaluate whether they were doing what you said you expected because they know of it, or because they think it's the right thing to do.

> **Much more damage is done to individuals when they are promoted above their skill capacity than is ever done by not promoting them early enough.**

Second, when watching markets react to advertising or sales efforts, it is essential to keep a careful tab on the original predictions and know when the data is contradicting the strategic targets and predictions. We all have a tendency to ignore results which contradict our expectations and forecasts. Many people change their views to fit the data which arise. They are not comfortable with results which contradict their predictions. Great leaders have no trouble with this because they differentiate between what is truly predictable and what must be accepted as haphazard outcomes. They also know that judgement only improves if properly tested and investigated, when wrong, in order to get it more accurate for the next time.

Third, when you have made assumptions within the strategic plans for political, governmental decisions, which you expect to affect the economy and make it go in a particular direction, it is always advisable to have an alternative plan ready when the politicians don't behave as predicted. Politicians and political events are the most difficult to predict for business leaders because politics deals in the currency of votes by people, which confer political power upon the politicians (in democratic countries anyway); whereas business people deal mainly with people voting with their wallets for goods and services which they can buy or not, it's a free choice.

For example: how would most business leaders have reacted if the Conservatives had been returned in the 1997 UK national election, rather than the Labour Party? How many unwise leaders had so totally committed their organization to the Labour Party that they would have been extremely embarrassed if the Conservatives had been returned to power?

Case study 5.5

FAILURE DISGUISED AS SUCCESS

A much-admired individual headed a major corporation with £7 billion revenue per annum and about £2 billion profit. I was asked to meet him by one of his subordinates, with whom I had worked for many years. We met over dinner and passed what was, for me, a dull evening. He told me nothing of substance about himself. He boasted a lot about his achievements. He never mentioned his private life, or anything that could make him sound human or interesting or a man who had succeeded in his life at anything other than being a famous and important leader.

Just one month later he was taken ill. He was off sick for six months. Even then, he returned prematurely to work, with drugs still needing to be pumped into him, day and night. He asked to see me and wondered whether he could talk 'his life' over with me. I agreed, although I had no idea what he wanted to discuss.

He told me that he was dreadfully unhappy. He and his wife had not liked each other since they married. I asked why? He told me that he had made an appalling business decision in his previous job. He had become personally liable for many millions of £s and had spent the past decade paying all his surplus income to lawyers and the creditors, to stave off

▶

adverse publicity and ignominy. His wife blamed him for subjecting their lives to such terrible pressure. Another consequence of that mistake was that, in spite of earning a substantial income for many years, he still had no savings and did not even own the roof over his family's head. His wife had stayed loyal throughout his sickness but now she wanted to divorce him and start a new life for herself.

We arranged to meet the following week. While I was driving towards his office he called me on my mobile phone. Don't come – I've some urgent company matters to attend to. I told him nothing could be more important than sorting out his marriage and his private life. But he cancelled anyway. He cancelled three more meetings before I gave up on him completely and realized it was pointless to put another appointment in my diary. A few weeks later he left work, sick, and never returned. He died a few months later, utterly alone.

Many people would regard his life as a substantial success. There may be measures that would count it as such. But I shall not be advocating any of them in this book.

THE POWER OF STUPIDITY

One of the phenomena I have always found utterly weird is how effective fools can be. People who are really, self-evidently stupid sometimes do the most amazingly effective things. Wise leaders should always be ready to learn from everybody, including fools. But they should also fear the power of stupidity. Fools can accidentally achieve clever things. Often this is because less bright people pursue their goals single-mindedly, because they are not clever enough to think of more than one goal at a time. For the intellectual leader, with a multitude of agendas and the power of conceptual thinking on many levels, the capacity of the single-minded fool to defeat them or prevent them from achieving their goals is very strong. Intellectually gifted people are particularly vulnerable to the power of stupidity. Fools can also do very stupid, nasty or

> One of the phenomena I have always found utterly weird is how effective fools can be.

dangerous things and damage you severely. One eminent but intellectually under-endowed leader I tried to help, agreed that all his executives (from around the world) needed to be more committed to delivering their budget promises, when they made their annual reviews. They had persistently failed to meet their promised targets for several years. At the end of a week of teaching the executives a series of case studies, demonstrating the need to commit to and deliver budget promises, this leader came in to make a speech saying, 'I know I promised the board £35 million profit this year. But they don't really expect it. I'll probably get away with £20m million. So we can all relax.' You can bet that results did not pick up! Stupidity is dangerous and worth avoiding if possible. I stopped trying to help this particular man. He did not survive much longer.

Excessive use of PR can prevent leaders from achieving their purposes

An advantage of a large corporate setting is that it often gives you attractive seeming opportunities to get into the media. The press, radio and television are omnipresent and easily available. It is tempting to use them. Apparently good reasons often present themselves – the best marketing books emphasize that PR is more effective than advertising. So it is easy to decide that the opportunity for self-promotion is for the good of the business. There are dangers associated with the use of publicity and the media that none of the text books will tell you. First, journalists love to build and then destroy. In many ways, they are like stockbrokers, they only make money out of turnover. So although they love good stories, they love bad ones even more. They will happily make you into a hero. The press will tell the world that your vision is unique, your executives love you and profits are enormous because you are a genius. Just as soon, they will return to tell the world you are a villain, your goods have killed children, your trucks ran over an old lady, your debts are mounting and yesterday's genius is today's idiot. It is not a conspiracy. It is how they sell newspapers. Their job is always to return to haunt you.

How does the seduction process take place? First, they invite you to remodel your instinctive business insight into a set of clichés to enable them to recount to the readers what you do, in language which the readers use but which you do not normally employ in business dealings. That forces you to express yourself in their thinking mode, not your own. In addition, they can easily start an addiction in you which works in a similar way to that of a drug. The addiction takes the form of needing to hear people start conversations with, 'I saw you on television last week'. When that excitement dies down after a few months, you begin to obsessively need another PR/media adrenaline kick. By now you will have learned the tricks of achieving media coverage. This is to issue a press release with any story – the first or the last time something happens, the largest or the smallest of anything or any other story a journalist can sell to his editor. You wrap up another of your ideas into a cliché. Pretty soon you are running your business along the lines of the clichés instead of with your original instinct and intuition. Thus you lose touch with your own business. You begin to believe your own mythology. Then you are on the slippery slope.

> **Rule: Never believe your own publicity.**

The same argument applies to awards for Business Person of the Year/Decade/Century. Why? They have the same effect described above. You have to turn your instinctive skills into clichés for the media. You'll end up taking decisions according to the lights of your clichés, not your instincts. Remember also that admiration from your peers soon turns to envy. It is advisable to ask yourself continuously whether your business will benefit from the award? Can it help your career? Awards such as Business Person of the Year serve little purpose other than to sell the media which promote them.

There are real benefits to keeping a low media profile. Bad luck and unfortunate incidents in your career will not be able to follow you around. By the way, never give credence to or discuss any unfortunate incidents in your career. That way, nobody will find it easy to use them against you. (Your enemies will always find good ammunition.) A lack of publicity makes it much easier for people to forget them. If, however, you do make an enemy inadvertently, don't ever fool yourself that they will forget the incident. People rarely do. It is far wiser not to make the enemy in the first place. Similarly, avoid crooks and immoral people. They always corrupt people who associate with them and their dirt rubs off. Unlike journalists, who follow a relatively honourable profession, the corruption in the soul of crooks always rubs off and damages people who associate with them.

In general, personal publicity is most useful as an example to others, at the close of a career, when one has no corporate goals to achieve but when one can pass wisdom on to the rising stars. It is probably the best time to theorize about what methods really worked for you, as a leader. It will also then be safe to admit your mistakes and what others might want to avoid.

Litmus tests

Litmus tests are the business equivalent of the litmus paper tests used in chemical science to measure for alkalinity or acidity. I have taken to setting up these litmus tests in most situations at senior level. They are vital when you doubt the sincerity of people you are involved with, or when you are assessing a leader's ability (check whether his or her first predictions come out) or when people *above all* are making claims to the ethical or moral high ground. It is also vital to create a litmus tests when implementing any decision, to check that the outcome evolves as predicted.

In my experience it is not advisable to allow too many counter indicators to your litmus tests. If people or events fail once or twice, change how you use those people immediately or change the resources going into the decision you have taken. It is important to act relatively fast when people fail their litmus tests. Consider, for example, the case of Lyam Strong at Sears. Towards the end of his tenure the stock analysts asserted he had the wrong strategy, yet his two chairmen and board of directors stuck with him. The poor shareholders lost a large percentage of the value of their original holding.

PERSUADING SHORT-TERM STAKEHOLDERS TO GET THINGS INTO PERSPECTIVE

A few years ago a managing director received the following letter from one of his regional directors, who was due to attend his annual performance and bonus review. It read as follows:

Dear Boss,

I am writing this letter from a hospital ward. I am waiting for the junior Transport Minister and local Member of Parliament, who was knocked down by our truck, to recover consciousness.

I should be able to attend next week's performance review, but that depends whether the Industrial Tribunal closes in time – you will remember we are defending a sexual harassment hearing of that secretary who had twins.

I may have to leave the review early because the local bank has asked to see me. There appears to be a discrepancy between the figures our accountant has sent Head Office and the actual cash banked.

No other worries at present, although I hope you don't mind if I stay overnight as a headhunter wants to speak to me. I'm only going because I'm not sure if it's about me or another of the senior team – but it's always best to go along and find out, I'm sure you'd agree.

I look forward to seeing you.

Yours sincerely

Fred

PS. Actually, boss, I just missed one budget target (I overspent on training by 1 per cent). I achieved all other objectives. I feel the team have performed tremendously and deserve their full bonus, which I am coming to the meeting to discuss. I just wanted to help you get things into perspective.

Good leaders keep things in perspective in their organization, both for themselves and their key personnel. No single manager is so important that his departure can damage the corporation. Very few single events can actually bring down the whole pack of tricks of the corporate state. Ensuring that everybody realizes this, and getting each

> **Good leaders keep things in perspective in their organization, both for themselves and their key personnel.**

event and happening into perspective, is an ability that all good leaders need.

By the way, one has to particularly admire leaders who also manage to persuade shareholders to 'keep things in perspective', often for years on end. I especially admire leaders of quoted companies who persuade shareholders to forgo dividends. In the long run it usually makes the shareholders much richer, although it also renders them less able to judge the performance of the organization. Few people are able to see clearly how much of the apparent capital gain is made at the expense of the forgone dividends!

DIFFERENT FORMS OF DECISION MAKING

This book is not meant to be a manual on decision making, more on leadership. However, it is worth putting in an *aide mémoire* for leaders on various concepts of decision making. First, inspect the matrix in Table 5.1 to get an overall view of the different forms of decision making and when they are applicable.

Table 5.1 Different decision making methods and when to use them

Decision-making type	Definition	Situations when most applicable
Zero-based	Taking the budget decisions for a new period as if there had been no previous history	Market undergoing rapid change Major new technology in the industry Competitors making rapid and deep inroads into the market When the executive in charge appears to be failing When the leader is considering hiving off the division and wishes to contain costs rigidly until a buyer is found
Incremental	Taking budget decisions on the basis of an incremental change rather than a radical reappraisal	In politics, in order to avoid upsetting constituents In most business decisions, because most of the business does not change from year to year When the stakeholders don't mind because you are delivering results within their comfort zone
Sub-optimal	Taking a decision which is not aiming to get a maximum result, rather it is aiming to achieve less than is feasible	When an organization has undergone radical change and needs a period of calm and achievement When the stakes are not high, nor the rewards When there is no right answer and it is *not* the moment to 'bet the company' When the shareholders are more than satisfied with current performance
Optimal	Taking a decision which is aiming to win the long-term future of the organization	When there is a strategic opportunity to achieve a winning position in an industry When the business is in danger of failure and only a major 'breakout' strategy will suffice When competitors are at a low ebb and could be taken out with the right optimal strategy

Table 5.1 continued

Decision-making type	Definition	Situations when most applicable
Maximiz-ing	Taking a decision to go for the highest possible profits or the greatest possible market share	When a technology breakthrough gives your organization a unique advantage over the competitors When your competitors are at a particularly low ebb and their cost structure is out of line When your management structure and development is running especially well When the leadership of your key competitors is weak or vulnerable When preparing the business for flotation or trade sale
Speedy and aggressive	Taking decisions with tight time constraints or to demonstrate aggression to competitors	When time is of the essence and your business has unique opportunities, such as limited patent life on high technology products or when the business has sole access to important ingredients of the supply mix When competitors are propitiously vulnerable When potential competitors are considering entering the market and you wish to warn them off

Zero-based decision-making

The zero-based budget decision making method approaches a situation or division or department from 'a state as if it did not exist at all'. It is particularly useful when examining parts of a business that look as if their marketplace is undergoing radical change, whether of growth or diminution. One has to make the assumption that the division does not exist and decide, in the light of as much new and old data as one can assemble, what resources should be put into that part of the organization, if any. Zero-based decision making techniques are usually thoroughly disliked by executives and staff alike because the method requires the questioning of every assumption and each allocation of resource. The process makes people feel extremely uncomfortable and often fearful. It can be highly disruptive and cause unexpected instability.

Incremental decision making

Aaron Wildavsky, a distinguished US academic, wrote his work (Wildavsky 1964) on the budgetary process mainly with politics in mind. He highlighted the fact that most decisions in government are governed by incremental decision making. That means that most political decisions are taken on the basis of a little change at any one time, usually between 5 per cent and 10 per cent. The same rules seem to apply to most business decisions. The majority of managers always offer about 5 per cent to 10 per cent better performance than last year. Most bosses only ask for that as well. Too often, both parties to the review set their annual budget with little reference to the prevailing market conditions and without considering thoroughly enough the true potential of demand for products and services.

> Most political decisions are taken on the basis of a little change at any one time, usually between 5 per cent and 10 per cent. The same rules seem to apply to most business decisions.

This also explains why the zero-based budget is often full of strife and is politically sensitive. Examining *everything* is the very opposite of incrementalism. It is very intimidating because managers fear they will lose far more with a zero-based examination of their part of the business than when they are asked for an incremental increase or decrease.

Sub-optimal decision making

This concept is discussed earlier. However, it is worth noting here that taking sub-optimal decisions may offer the best solution after one has taken account of all the available options. This seeming paradox gains verisimilitude with an example. The market for cable television in the UK has consistently performed below expectations. Leaders of businesses in the industry seem unable to decide whether the causes are either that the British just don't like TV enough or that the prices are too high. If the latter, then the economics of the industry don't work. It could be that the market is just taking longer to evolve. The industry also has problems because its supply chain is imprisoned by the iron grip of a supplier with short-term profit-maximizing tendencies (BSkyB). Meanwhile, businesses in the industry have the opportunity to keep themselves above water by focusing upon their telephony business where another dominant firm (British Telecom) is controlled by its regulator (and is also more circumspect and long-sighted about exploiting its market dominance). In circumstances like these, there is no perfect or right solution to the strategic questions faced by leaders in the industry. Sub-optimality becomes the prevailing wisdom and the safest route to a solution which will emerge from the marketplace, some time in the future.

Optimal decision making

Optimal decision making is about taking a decision which is aiming to win the long-term future of the organization. It means getting everything right, the stakeholders, the economics of the industry, the timing and the opportunity. It requires a high quality team to be at the peak of its form and working at their best with the leader. The situations when optimal decision making are required are not frequent. When they go well, however, there is enormous satisfaction. The times when optimality is needed are few, but they will include situations such as a strategic opportunity to achieve a winning position in an industry or when the business is in danger of bankruptcy and only a major 'breakout' strategy will enable it to escape the liquidator. Occasionally the leader might judge that the competitors are at a low ebb and could be taken out with the correct optimal strategy. This is always a dangerous assumption because competitors are rarely as stupid or sleepy as one assumes.

Decision making aiming for a maximum result

It is always a key condition of going for the maximum that your management structure and development should be running especially well.

Taking a maximizing decision means going for either the highest possible profits or the greatest possible market share. It is always a high-risk procedure because it often leaves little margin for error. It also has the unfortunate side effect of setting up the leader for failure, if they achieve anything less than the maximum they are aiming at. Most leaders wisely avoid such situations. Occasions when the maximum may be an appropriate objective will be, for example, when a technology breakthrough has given your organization a unique advantage over its competitors, or when your competitors are at a particularly low ebb and their cost structure is out of line (they may be locked into a bad contract, for example), or when their leadership is weak or vulnerable. It is always a key condition of going for the maximum that your management structure and development should be running especially well. Finally, leaders will often aim for a maximizing result when preparing a business for flotation on a stock exchange, or for a trade sale. The maximum result will also maximize the value of the business.

Speedy and aggressive decision making

Speedy and aggressive decision making is appropriate when the opportunities and the prizes in the marketplace are especially high. Aggression is not usually recommended because it implies excessive force. Exploiting strategic force often brings out the worst retaliation from the competitors. However, there are times when a leader has to go for the main chance. It often seems to be most applicable to industries such as pharmaceuticals and, sometimes, high technology industries such as IT, software and hardware, consumer entertainment systems, modern chip-based gadgetry, etc. One often finds that it is the prime mover in businesses in these industries, under modern conditions of vast levels of necessary investment, who wins the day. Usually an aggressive form of decision making is most appropriate under those circumstances. It should be speedy decision making, too, because this is appropriate when the market is developing fast and therefore necessitates aggressive decision making in the first place. There is no point in being aggressive and going for it, if one does not also do it fast and try to beat the competition into the shops or where ever the marketplace requires distribution.

Communicating decisions

Great leaders know that taking the decision is just the start. Like strategy analysis itself, the process and the choices are relatively easy. It's the quality of implementation that ruins the outcome of the decisions. The first job to do after taking a decision is to communicate it to all the necessary interested parties. Of course, much of the communicating should have taken place before the decision gets ratified formally, because the leader would have consulted many people in the organization while assembling the data to take the decision. Normally, the only exception to this will be mergers or takeovers, where secrecy is a formal and legal requirement of the authorities that govern such matters. When it comes to communications, the size of the organization is the key guideline to the required methods and channels. Very large businesses with 100 000 or more employees require the use of the most modern communications techniques. The leader should probably use video film or telecommunications or radio links to all the relevant sites where their employees are massed. In the case of international businesses of that size, a minimum is the use of telephone-conferencing, although televised telephone-conferencing is getting cheaper all the time and can be more effective if the leader understands and has mastered the techniques of the medium. By and large, it is a good idea to avoid paperwork and bureaucracy. In general, the less paper that emanates from the office of the chair or CEO, the better.

For businesses between 50 000 and 100 000 employees it is probably still feasible for leaders to try to retain some personal presence, by going to the actual sites and talking to their people personally. It is particularly important when major decisions are being taken and need to be communicated. It should be built into the diary as an absolute. There are always many spurious reasons why visiting the sites to talk to your employees seems less important than meeting all the apparently important and interesting to talk to City analysts, bankers, journalists and consultants. However, those external advisers rarely make money for your business. The workers do. Go see them on site, where they work.

When important decisions are in the process of being taken, it is important not to communicate too soon. Early exposure can ruin a decision, particularly if it is controversial. It may raise the hackles of so many people that it ensures enough anger is aroused to guarantee the failure of the decision when you do eventually get approval from the board to implement it. Once the decision is taken, communicating it clearly to the right people is the key to acceptance. I have learned from experience that going through the correct procedures of etiquette and good manners is a great discipline and often helps ensure that you get it right. This will apply equally with regard to your behaviour with your board of directors as well as outside parties such as regulators and merchant bankers (with whom you may have covenant agreements on their loans to the business). The same correct procedures should also apply in your dealings with the 'wrong' people, such as competitors or suppliers (before workers) or bankers (when they have no stopping power or prior rights on the use of your capital).

Giving the right message is vital – try to visualize what you are saying and also its reception, so that you ensure that the words you use communicate what you intend them to mean. Although this sounds simplistic, I am astonished how frequently even excellent communicators fail to think about how to transmit their message clearly. It is always advisable to rehearse well, no matter how long you've been doing it. People hearing the messages manage to find very creative ways of misunderstanding the meaning and seeing the communication in a way which contradicts utterly the intention of the communicator. Peoples' capacity for multiple interpretation of the same set of words is vast. Wise leaders never underestimate the problem and always check to see how their messages have been received and what, exactly, people understood. It can be a salutary exercise.

Monitoring the consequences of decisions

All good leaders make strong assertions (at least to themselves) and set up litmus tests of their predictions about the future. They will do the same about any decision they make about the organization and how it will cope with and react to their decisions. They will know how to react if a decision's consequences don't turn out as they predict. Taking remedial action early enough is as important as trying to get the decisions right in the first place. They will also monitor the external environment carefully, to check whether their predictions about the future come out as forecast. Top-notch leaders accept when they are wrong (or the environment refuses to co-operate) and change their decision to match the changed circumstances. Sometimes they may have to admit that the original decision was just plain wrong and needs to be changed or improved upon.

> Top-notch leaders accept when they are wrong (or the environment refuses to co-operate) and change their decision to match the changed circumstances.

Leaders need to get their decisions right most of the time – but not all the time! Demanding perfection in a leader is too formidable a requirement! However, when they do get it wrong they must know how to recognize it, be prepared to accept it and put it right as quickly as possible. This also means that a misplaced ego is definitely *not* a leadership skill. Nor is arrogance, nor a lack of humility. The organization's interests should always remain paramount. If they are not, both the leader and the business are likely to be in danger.

When leaders fail to offer strong predictions about the outcomes of their larger-scale decisions, their board should force them to do so. If the leader still manages to avoid offering litmus test-type predictions to the board, the directors should put in their own predictions instead. However, when they do, they must monitor with data, truth and facts, not politics, rumour and gossip. The board should also ensure that the rewards and bonuses it offers the leader are aimed at fulfilling the decisions and outcomes they have backed. Only too often, sly managers subtly adapt their predictions and promises into other measures and objectives which resemble more closely what is being achieved rather than what was promised. When leaders do not deliver, bonuses should not be paid. Furthermore, appropriate reactions should be installed and implemented instead.

CHANGING YOUR MIND

Good leaders change their minds! That is a given absolute. But under what circumstances is it permissible or appropriate? First, when external events turn out differently to their predictions or forecasts. A second reason for changing one's mind may be because the human resources of the organization proved unfit to implement the decisions (this would, of course, mean that the original decision making was of dubious quality and judgement). Unpredictable trauma and events can change the data. Examples could be a takeover bid emerging, a technological breakthrough by a rival competitor, or a major stock market crash reducing the general availability of capital. Sometimes competitors behave unreasonably, unpredictably or stupidly (although 'stupidity' in a competitor often means that they were cleverer than you!). Some things cannot easily be predicted, such as the leader becoming unwell. It may decided to change the decision to give the organization more chance of success, in the light of the leader's poor health. Sometimes other key people leave the business or fall ill, although no strategy for a medium-sized or large business should ever be too dependent on a single individual. New technology or innovations sometimes change the given data of the industry. Other events which cannot be predicted might be political interference; unpredictable action(s) from regulators who change the rules of the game; or 'acts of god' such as bad or good weather, which has large effects upon annual sales of drinks, food, and fuel businesses.

The one area in which leaders should never change their minds is over ethical or moral issues, where somebody has broken agreed ethical codes or an organizational process has led the business into behaving unjustly to an individual. This rule should be changed only when the leader finds they have failed to think through all the consequences of an ethical code or a new situation forces them to realize they had not understood its principles properly.

THE SHORT-TERM CONSIDERATIONS OF LEADERS

It was stated above that there is no excuse for any leader not to deliver short-term as well as long-term results. A young manager on the way to the top never knows how long they will be in any particular job. They should always try to make a difference early, based on long-term principles of good management, which will be a precursor to their eventual leadership style. This section sets out the type of controls to which any competent young manager and potential leader will give their attention in the short term, to ensure that positive results come through early. They have to examine the control of short-term costs. These should include everything on the following list, at the very least:

- the use of temporary staff
- any wasteful use of company cars and the fuel that goes in them
- excessive use of hire vehicles and taxis
- invoices for fast messenger and parcel delivery services
- excess property that is not being exploited or rented out
- property renewal projects that may be unnecessary
- new IT being installed without viable commercial reasons
- excessive numbers of secretaries and personal assistants
- all regular payments of fees to outside consultants
- costs of company canteens
- all subsidized or regular supplies of food and beverages for staff and workers
- all standing orders or direct debits
- subscriptions for newspapers or magazines
- any other subscription services that may not have been reviewed for some time.

A ruthless review of the items mentioned above will guarantee, in any large business, the possibility of making considerable savings and short-term profit effects (or at least avoidance of waste). It is always worthwhile examining attitudes towards human resources. This is an area where the greatest laxness prevails because it is human nature not to confront people issues.

One short-term concern of leaders should be to continuously monitor any matters arising from current fashion and short-term trends. A leader should always be assessing whether something represents a passing fad or a genuine long-term trend. Similar considerations apply to short-term changes in demographics (more working women available, subsidies for employing youths, etc.). Leaders need to differentiate between evolving fashions which may give opportunities to make some short-term profits, and other 'fads' which are irrelevant as a business opportunity.

> **A leader should always be assessing whether something represents a passing fad or a genuine long-term trend.**

LEADERS' LONG-TERM CONSIDERATIONS

There appear to be certain subjects that most leaders keep to the forefront of their minds, as key indicators and potential scenario material for their thinking about the leadership decisions they have to make. Often one such key factor is the trend in long-term interest rates. These affect everything to do with the cost structure of any business, whether it is managing its own investment funds or investing in capital for future manufacturing. Similarly, the rate of inflation can be a leading trend indicator, but for different reasons. Inflation is a great distorter of information. Poorly performing companies can use inflationary figures to cover up their failure to produce real profits. This phenomenon was prevalent towards the end of the highly inflationary 1980s. During that period, businesses which had not traded profitably for years and which had been dressing up their inflated revenues to look like profits suddenly saw all their chickens come home to roost – their profits disappeared as the inflation rate returned to normal levels and their businesses died.

Leaders need to pay careful attention to the long-term economics of their particular industry and the organization they are leading. In the long run, no matter how clever they may be, nor how brilliant their chosen strategy, no leader can beat the objective facts of economics and the demand curve. If customers won't buy the service you are offering at the prices you need to charge to make a profit, you cannot remain in the market. We discussed the cable television industry earlier in this chapter. This is exactly their problem. The people in the industry do not know whether they face a different demand curve in the UK compared to that in the USA, where the demand for the service is proven (although not highly profitable except to the founding owners). The long-term trends of the products and services of the organization must be monitored and continuously evaluated to judge where the long-term direction of the demand curves are headed. This will be the prime indicator to judge potential long-term profitability. Good leaders also take time to install tools to analyze the nature of true economic value, compared to short-term, less substantive profits. Although we argue above that good leaders will know how to produce immediate, short-term profits, as well as long-term economic value, they should always take steps to ensure that not too many short-term profit-appearance-creating tricks are being played on them. These might include managers failing to spend marketing budgets, not using their budget allocations of human resource training, failures to repair buildings properly (thus developing long-term legal liabilities), over-extending the company car leasing arrangements to save taking 'hits' on residual vehicle values and the many other ploys that managers exploit to assure their bonuses and promotions.

Good leaders focus upon the long-term development of people, particularly development programmes for future leaders, graduate entry programmes and the development of middle management. Wise leaders also never neglect plain old training for other workers and staff. Noel Tichy, a University of Michigan professor and a consultant, has found that really successful organizations concentrate on producing a 'leadership engine' which produces high quality leadership skills in all the junior, middle and senior managers of a business. Organizations should not rely on having one of the few great leaders around. When they create a development and mentoring ambiance throughout the organization, with all the leaders taking responsibility for developing people pro-actively, the business creates a resilience which safeguards those times when new top leaders are settling in or when they are just not the best of the type.

Another factor in good leadership is the choice of quality subordinates. There is probably no other single variable that can make or break a leader's career than the ability to select, appoint and retain quality people. Many successful people have claimed, 'I don't need to be good. I just surround myself with good people!' Alongside these good people, it is always advisable to install a mentoring system, so that the best among the leadership group can choose subordinates in the organization to mentor. This ensures that the best people are being brought on and the succession is being prepared. Of course, there is a supplementary advantage to mentoring systems – they keep leaders in touch with live projects going on around the business and ensure that any necessary warning signals about the quality of succession planning are being monitored and reacted to. Great leaders also pay heed to the organization of succession to themselves. A good leader succeeded by an idiot becomes, in retrospect, a poor leader. If the business is going to fall to pieces as soon as they leave because they were too 'great' to have good people around them ready to succeed, they have no right to the title 'great' at all.

> **A good leader succeeded by an idiot becomes, in retrospect, a poor leader.**

This also raises the question of how one might expect a good leader to deal with rivals for their own position. If a rival is worthy, some choose to encourage them at a distance. However, the wisest leaders I know often choose a different course of action and keep their rivals close to hand. That way they can measure their rival's ambition against their own knowledge and wisdom. If the rival is really good they will not endanger the leader. If they are even better, a truly wise person would put them in charge and take an appropriate bonus for doing so, after having given them testing responsibilities. As they succeed, they can promote them fast. You won't want a high-quality personal rival working for the competition and you need to discover just how good they are. Prepare them for succession. You might find they are just too good for your organization because the business does not have enough potential for their talent. In that case, send then to another organization to give them the future they deserve. Of course, if, upon testing, they prove unworthy, there are other choices. They may be unworthy but nice –

most leaders I know send these types of people to work in the human resources department (to give them better quality self-appraisal skills). If they are nevertheless of value to the organization, though, not as a potential successor, then they need to be developed to make the best use of their skills for the business. If they have few redeeming features, dismiss them. If they are really nasty, give them a superb résumé and send them to work for the competition!

Good leaders always pay attention to the ratio between fixed and variable costs. The former are always dangerous because they cannot be managed away easily. Markets and customers move much more fluidly and the more variable the costs of the business, the more the organization can react to its markets. Wise leaders always try to minimize fixed costs or render them more variable. Variable costs are always a preferable form of overhead because these maximize the flexibility of the organization's capacity to adapt to any external circumstances.

Finally, in my experience leaders always monitor long run demographic trends. These provide the vital indicators about potential future employees and customers. If one understands what people want in the long run, one has the necessary information on how to survive and thrive. Such data will link closely to the classical marketing information which all leaders observe, such as long-run consumer tastes, technological breakthroughs in associated and non-associated industries, and the long-run nature of consumer trends themselves. If you do not know what the consumers of the 21st century are going to want, no matter what sector your business is in you will, sooner or later, lose touch with their potential effects upon your business.

SUMMARY

This chapter has examined different forms of decision making and in what circumstances each might be appropriately employed. These forms are not just for leaders at the top of a business but for every aspiring leader to learn to exploit and select when they find themselves in the right situation. Although most leadership decision making should be about the longer term, there will be many occasions for the rising executive who is destined to become a leader to have to take short-term decisions with long-term effects. I have set out above a brief outline of stakeholder theory, as originally examined by Professor Herbert Simon, and drawn out the implications this has for retaining perspective, helicoptering and learning to make balanced decisions. This chapter has also covered the relevant factors to high quality decision making in terms of personal capacity and organizational situation. Chapter 6 will further develop some of the qualities it takes to rise to the heights of organizational leadership.

RECOMMENDED READING FOR CHAPTER 5

Braybrooke, D. and Lindblom, C. D. (1969) *A Strategy of Decision*. Glencoe: Free Press.

Hamel, G. and Prahalad, C. K. (1994) *Competing for the Future*. Cambridge, MA: Harvard Business School Press.

Herder, J. (1992) *The Tao of Leadership*. Aldershot: Gower.

Hickson, D. J. *et al.* (1986) *Top Decisions*. Oxford: Basil Blackwell.

Kakabadse, A. (1991) *The Wealth Creators*. London: Kogan Page.

Jaques, E. (1976) *A General Theory of Bureaucracy*. London: Heinemann.

Jaques, E. (1982a) *The Form of Time*. London: Heinemann.

Jaques, E. (1982b) *Free Enterprise, Fair Employment*. London: Heinemann.

Lawrence, P. R. and Lorsch, J. W. (1967) *Managing Integration and Differentiation* Cambridge: Harvard University Press.

March, J. G. (1988) *Decisions and Organizations*. Oxford: Basil Blackwell.

Peter, L. J. and Hull, R. (1979) *The Peter Principle*. London: Pan.

Peters, T. J. and Waterman, R. H., Jr. (1982) *In Search of Excellence*. New York: Harper & Row.

Tichy, N. M. and Cohen, E. (1997) *The Leadership Engine*. New York: Harper Business.

Wildavsky, A. (1964) *The Politics of the Budgetary Process*. Boston: Little Brown.

Biographies of companies and leaders

Eberts, J. and Ilott, T. (1990) *My Indecision is Final*. London: Faber & Faber.

Gittin, N. and Masters, K. (1997) *Hit and Run*. New York: Simon & Schuster.

Lenzner, R. (1985) *The Great Getty*. New York: Signet.

Malik, R. (1975) *And Tomorrow the World?* London: Millington.

Maney, K. (1995) *Megamedia Shakeout*. New York: John Wiley.

McLachlan, S. (1983) *The National Freight Buy-Out*. London: MacMillan.

Shawcross, W. (1992) *Murdoch*. London: Chatto & Windus.

Sloan, A. P. (1965) *My Years with General Motors*. New York: MacFadden-Bartell.

Thompson, P. (1990) *Sharing the Success*. London: Fontana.

Walton, S. (1993) *Made in America*. New York: Bantam.

Wanstell, G. (1987) *Tycoon*. London: Grafton.

LEADERSHIP, CREATIVITY AND EVOLUTION

Creativity in a leader takes a different form to that of the managers and executives who work for them. This chapter examines the balance between using one's own innovative strategic or lateral thinking skills rather than those of other managers. I will suggest ways of maintaining or increasing your powers of creativity and how to use other people's lateral thinking to best advantage for the organization

NORMAL CREATIVITY AND LEADERSHIP

A standard definition of creativity and creative thinking is that creative thinkers 'think out of the box'. They are able to come up with genuinely fresh ideas from within themselves. In terms of the Belbin team-skills test, discussed above, they are the 'plants' of a team, because when you *plant* somebody with these skills in a team, that whole team starts to be more creative. That is not the creativity that leaders usually have or need. People with the 'plant' skill often lack interpersonal skills and also tend to lack judgement about other people's ideas as compared to their own. They are not skilled team players, often needing help to communicate their ideas. They need a chairperson who knows how to use them and maintain their self esteem and flow of ideas. The chairperson is more likely to be the leader, whose special creativity comes from their ability to take the best ideas from the 'plant', assess the other skills of the team, analyze the external market situation, judge the attitudes of all the stakeholders and then take an optimal decision on behalf of the business. That is the special skill that I believe it is right to call the *creativity of leadership*.

Does a leader need any creativity?

The creativity of leaders is different because it's strategic. They can create a corporate mission statement that looks clever to the brightest people among their City and investing stakeholders, yet can also act as a clear guideline to every member of staff who needs the mission statement to know where the company is going and when. The leaders' creativity scans the total external environment, often around the globe; they discover new opportunities; they apprehend fresh dangers; and they have the creative ability to decide when to take advantage of the opportunities and how to avoid the dangers. They will examine the inner workings of the organization and know how to exploit the internal strengths and culture and how to repair the weaknesses. They will appreciate the core competencies of the business and know what needs additional resources. When all this data is assembled, a great leader will begin the process of innovative strategic creativity.

After deciding, creatively, what to do, the leader then has to find ways of communicating it in a digestible form to the full range of recipients, both bright and less so. This also requires a special kind of creativity. Great leaders do it and we don't even see the strain.

What form does leadership creativity take?

The creativity we are describing here is not defined in anything the current text books describe. None the less, it is a special form of creativity and only great leaders have it.

They must be creative about all the strategic aspects of the organization. Whatever they do, the expenditure they authorize, the way they spend their time, or the attitudes they display to staff and customers, all the examples they set are the consequence of creative strategic thought, applied to establishing a safe, profitable and long-lasting future for the organization. Their creativity is a continuous stream of thought, behaviour and action, always focused on the strategic health and benefit of the business. They are being creative when thinking and while doing all their work for the business. Their behaviour *needs* to be creative, setting exemplars and showing their staff how to behave and what to do. The way they react to news and results and how they adjust the organization's administrative processes to every piece of relevant data – requires creativity.

Ultimately, the key ingredients to the creativity of great leadership seem to be a series of paradoxes and counterbalancing dynamics. I describe it, therefore, with the following paradoxes:

- utterly lateral yet firmly based and grounded
- creative but appearing to be mundane (after the event)
- complex yet simple in their aggregation of the data
- simplicity emerging from mental brightness
- customer-focused yet with careful regard to the workers
- utterly individualistic while based on everybody's best generalized thinking
- with one swoop they cover both the short and the long term
- their actions induce the thought, 'why didn't I think of that?'
- although based on complexity, their ideas can be explained very simply.

Although I have often asked, leaders rarely seem to know where their inspiration comes from. 'It's just there', they usually say.

> Some leaders have the appearance of knowing how to create value because they understand how to manipulate investment criteria and stock markets. But this is the creation of monetary value only. What I am referring to is the creation of true economic value for workers and consumers, the true *creation of wealth*, not *nominal money value*.

How can leaders ensure that they have sufficient and appropriate creativity?

This begs the question, 'can creativity be created or is it just there?' Again, we come close to the question posed by the title of this book. Is the leader born with creativity or can it be developed in business schools or by consultants with training programmes? Ultimately it is a vital part of the leadership role, that a leader must be able to create and take the right decisions on behalf of the organization. If they cannot summon that type of creativity (whether they use others in a team, or particular individuals) then they cannot be said to be fit for the purposes of leadership. Thus, by definition, a great or good leader must have the necessary strategic creativity, or know how to assemble the creative elements to enable him to exercise his or her judgement to take full responsibility for the ultimate decisions that the role demands.

Table 6.1 The balanced dynamics of leadership creativity

The creative leadership dynamic	Creative effect
Rounded and balanced	Sees all sides of the strategic picture
Objective rather than subjective	Takes objectively optimal balanced decisions
Capable of dispassion	While retaining humanity, takes decisions in the best interests of the business
Always seeing a bigger picture than those around him	Self-confidently knowing they are best suited to take the decision
Emotionally mature and naïve	Understands the human aspects but sees clearly what is important and ignores the rest
Wise rather than clever	Uses whole range of intelligence and emotional maturity rather than IQ alone
An individual rather than a team player	Having served management time as a good team player, as a leader their individuality is the premium that makes the difference
More character than personality	Not sidetracked by the ephemerality of personality, more endowed with the *gravitas* of character

A FIRST SET OF BALANCES AND TRADE-OFFS

Rounded and balanced

A rounded person sees the world around them 'with balance and circumspection'. They understand that, when people and events are going well, there is likely to be a compensating downturn. They know that most aspects of life have balancing factors. The rounded person is neither optimistic nor pessimistic; not a party pooper nor the person who occupies the centre of attraction. They are grounded and stable, while still being capable of joy.

'Roundedness' describes the kind of maturity needed by leaders. To be rounded, a leader will have reached a point in their life where they see things 'in the round', with circumspection. Leaders need to be rounded to ensure that they can use their sense of balance to helicopter above both the people and the data that surround important decisions. Their balance is an accessory to their roundedness, because they still have to align themselves somewhere on the decision making spectrum. When they do, it must be in a balanced position.

Objective rather than subjective

Although the leader must be thoroughly human and retain the subjectivity of their humanity, they also need to be able, at the moment of final decision taking, to be totally objective in their decision, which cannot be influenced by personal interests or idiosyncratic likes and dislikes. I remember a certain leader I admired appointing one of his people who was a delightful companion, but who was also, unfortunately an alcohol-dependent and strategically blind no-hoper. However, they played golf together and liked each other. It was a terrible mistake. He put him in charge of the best-performing division. It soon became the worst.

Capable of dispassion

This is different from the concept of objectivity, because it contains the idea that leaders must have a cold centre, a capacity for cutting off totally from the cutting edge of the organization. It is a capacity of not belonging, an ability to not be there. It is an observation that has been made of many of the most creative and successful leaders. At times they stand so completely apart from everything around them that their dispassion is both tangible and fearsome.

Always seeing the bigger picture

The leader has to retain the ability, when the chips are down, to see the bigger picture. It is something all great leaders have in common. It is a trick that enables them to create situations whereby their organization always wins, whatever the outcome. For an example, see Case study 6.1.

Case study 6.1

I KNEW A LEADER ONCE ...

I knew another leader once who was completely raw in his leadership skills, had not yet learned strategic insight, found it hard to take decisions, did not know about City institutions and was manipulated continuously by his fairly unpleasant corporate masters; but I liked him because he had promise ... and I wondered.

Early in our relationship he realized that he would have to find some independent capital for his business if he was to escape his controlling shareholders. We found a finance director who also knew the institutions which could lend him the money to become independent. His corporate controllers told him they did not want him to appoint an FD until they had considered the matter for six months or a year. This meant he would have lost the best candidate and would have delivered so much value to his owners that he would have little value left to float the company upon, when they would be ready, finally, to let him float.

The solution? Appoint the potential FD as a consultant, with a promise that, one way or another, he would be FD when the leader had permission or independence to appoint whomever he liked. This way he could tell his corporate controllers that he had obeyed. If they were sincere in their 'need to consider' they would not object to any choice made. If they were insincere the leader needed this individual in place to ensure that he could get finance when needed from the merchant bankers where the potential FD had connections. The objective was to be in a winning position whether his masters were playing false or true, manipulating or merely procrastinating.

Emotionally mature and naïve

This is a strangely contrasting set of qualities a leader needs, to ensure that their creativity is retained. Emotional maturity is about being grown up and accepting of all aspects of oneself. In his book *Games People Play* (Berne 1968) Eric Berne wrote about the three aspects of personal evolution in humans – child, parent, and adult. What many people do not understand is that one can and should retain aspects of all three throughout life. This is often a difficult thing for children to accept. They usually want their parents to remain either as parents or as adults, often not being sure which they really prefer or want. (Probably parents when they need help and adults when they don't.) But to be a leader you need to be an adult most of the time because your

> Leaders have to ask the vital breakthrough question, which creates in others the inspiration to come up with the new product or see a hitherto disguised new market.

people need to be treated as mature adults in their own right. You also need to remain a child so that you can see the world with fresh and naïve eyes. Children always ask 'why' and 'why not?' – great leaders do the same. Leaders have to ask the vital breakthrough question, which creates in others the inspiration to come up with the new product or see a hitherto disguised new market. Akio Morita, an early leader of Sony, the global electronics business, used to say, 'I don't do market research to find out what the public might want. It is my job to imagine things they can never dream of, create them and then delight them with a product they wondered how they ever managed without.'

Wise rather than clever

We have discussed elsewhere the difference between wisdom and cleverness. Wisdom is the profound insight that beats the quick wits of cleverness at every turn. Wisdom is the profound ability to have insight into multiple agendas, to understand with the heart and the head at the same time. Wisdom enables a leader to allow weakness and failure in subordinates and still not lose an appreciation of their qualities and value. When it comes to creativity, wisdom is vital, because it informs the leader how to be both the adult and the child, how to be both objective and subjective, how to both creative and analytical and, ultimately, to know what to decide to arrive at the optimum solution.

An individual rather than a team player

It is a feature of most leaders that they know how to join in with team work and how to be both a leader and a follower in a team. They will have had a normal management career, during which the teamwork of management would have been a vital skill. Ultimately, however, most great

> **It is a feature of most leaders that they know how to join in with team work and how to be both a leader and a follower in a team.**

leaders are not committed team players. This is caused partly by the very fact of leadership. In becoming a leader, they have had to separate themselves from the team and become more independent in their thinking and feeling. It is also a quality of leaders that they are detached (as we have seen) and that they retain a part of them that is free from teams and associations. It is the part of themselves that ensures they become a leader rather than a team player. In politics, in the UK, there was the famous example of Rab Butler, who was a great supporting minister to two prime ministers, Sir Anthony Eden and Harold Macmillan, and was considered to be 'the greatest prime minister Britain *never* had'. He was the ultimate team player, not a leader. And when it came to the special hunger for the top job, he just did not 'have what it takes' to grasp the prize.

More 'character' than personality

This subject has also been discussed in Chapter 4. Suffice to remark here that when it comes to creativity, character is much more important than personality. The latter gets in the way of the creative purpose. It distorts because it looks for the casual and superficial. Leaders with character bide their time, let others make their inputs, and then catalyze the decision making process to a successful outcome.

WHAT KIND OF PERSON SHOULD A LEADER BE?

A leader has to be natural. An artificial presence can prevent the leader from being natural, balanced, and rounded. Leaders need each of those qualities, because if they have to waste energy constraining their natural selves then the necessary freedom to be creative and intuitive will be destroyed. Creativity and intuition demand equilibrium and neutrality. They require the leader to be relatively objective in their judgements. Thus, although great leaders do not need to be perfect, one must ask, 'what qualities must they have to be assessed as a great leader', and to be effective in the role of leadership? They need to know how to take the organization into new industries and to ever-greater heights of achievement than its constituent members thought possible. The leader needs to be strategic, visionary, attractive, and fun to work for. Above all, the leader needs to be creative, in my special sense, because creativity is the vital catalyst for the creation of wealth, excitement and fun. Creativity is one of the special attributes which give meaning to life. How can leaders ensure that, in spite of their weaknesses, their Achilles' heels, they remain creative and are thus able to create wealth? Those qualities are summarized by a series of paradoxical balancing antitheses – trade-offs between two ends of a spectrum of skills. There are, in addition, some vital and necessary talents that become a *sine qua non* for creativity. This chapter will not contain all the answers because nobody has them. Each great leader is a unique construct. But I will try to cover the available range and the necessary qualities of which the mix may be composed. The balancing dynamic is composed of the elements shown in Table 6.1 above, which has already been discussed in detail on pp. 182–6 above.

The vital skills of leaders

Leaders need to understand how to handle people. This seems so trite one is almost embarrassed to write it. But it needs stating. One of the important differences between nominal and strategic leaders, is that the latter understand people and the former don't. Strategic leaders understand how people react to decisions and news. They see what is not obvious, when people are hurt or weighed down by personal problems. They also accept weaknesses as a part of the fabric of corporate society.

A leader also needs a subtle understanding of how people 'hear' communications. They know they need to say the same thing a thousand times, in many different ways, at every level of the organization, to thoroughly communicate important ideas as well. In the creative process, they pull out the best contributions from everybody. In addition to verbal ability, the leader in the modern era also requires a facility with numerical skills (all businesses measure themselves and are measured by others with numbers). Likewise, most great strategic ideas need to be tested arithmetically for their impact on the market and their value on the bottom line for the business. Numbers can become a creative medium for those leaders who think mathematically rather than verbally.

An ability to assess people and their skills accurately is important. One needs to be able to focus upon a person's best qualities and make people realize that one cares about them. It is sometimes said, cynically, that the ability to imitate sincerity is one of the highest leadership art forms. Perhaps the ability of leaders to retain distance creates this impression while still caring for their people all the time.

Leaders who inspire people to strive for and make achievements beyond their imagination are also creators of immense job satisfaction for others. They can also do it for themselves. Great leaders have the ability to undertake highly concentrated activity at intense pressure. In the present era, with vast communication capacity and the ability to move large amounts of capital around the world almost instantaneously, both crises and opportunities arise with little warning. It could be a take over bid or an opportunity to gain a licence to develop the business's products in a vast market like China. It might be one of the businesses going into a sudden meltdown (following currency problems or a balance of payments deficit, for example). Whatever the cause, the need inevitably arises that one has to react fast, and devote oneself intensively to a particular problem for a period. If one does not have the necessary powers of concentration and stamina at these times, one will fail at the first crisis. Crises can make and break a leadership career. Great leaders are always ready to meet their Waterloo. By the way, if you find you are having too many Waterloos each year, you should be thinking about whether this is related to your leadership skills or to the need for a deputy to be fielding some of the flak.

> It is sometimes said, cynically, that the ability to imitate sincerity is one of the highest leadership art forms.

You also need to know when to relax. This will be necessary both between and even during the crises. If you cannot control yourself enough to relax for some time each day, you are not going to remain fit for the important battles and wars. I remember one nominal leader, who boasted to me that he spent nearly $10 000 on telephone charges while on a ten day cruise on a ship, with his wife, for what was meant to be a holiday. He believed it was impressive that he had stayed in touch with his businesses while on holiday. Both his boss and I were so deeply unimpressed by his silly boast that we both decided that little could be done to help him improve his leadership skills (which was the job I was meant to be doing for him on behalf of his boss) when he was still behaving like that at the age of 53.

Last, but equally important, every leader needs multilevel listening skills. This refers to the ability that many leaders have to listen to differing messages, carrying a multitude of meanings from different types of people at every level in the organization. This skill is also used to understand the multiple agendas from the same set of messages, that are often being delivered to leaders whenever people communicate with them.

The traits and skills of leaders

I am differentiating between *traits* from *skills* by the distinction that skills are necessary whereas traits are useful and indicative. Skills are abilities and techniques that the leaders need to have at their disposal. Traits are characteristics and mannerisms which tend to be associated with many leaders, but cannot be considered essential in the same way that some skills emphatically are.

For example, a fine trait, for a leader, is not to need to dominate people, situations, in rooms, or at meetings. By contrast, it is a leadership skill to know how and when to dominate a room or discussion. It is a trait to have presence without noise, and a tendency to be more of a listener than a talker. It is a skill to ensure that one knows how to be heard, whenever it is necessary, to make an important point. Wise leaders often have the trait of exuding confidence in their subordinate's ability to achieve objectives while never falsely making any job seem too easy or too hard. The skill of presenting challenges to their subordinates, directly and with honesty, is a *sine qua non*. By transmitting their belief in the person's ability to accomplish the objectives they are setting they, somehow, add to the subordinate's self-belief and confidence that they can actually achieve the job they are given. The leader's belief in them becomes a function of their belief in themselves.

Leaders are capable of understanding the essence of every part of the business without a need to have technical competence. For example: they need to understand how IT can be exploited to do things for the organization, without needing to speak the language of gigabytes and ram or to demonstrate technical ability in order to take the decisions.

Skills and traits leaders don't need

> **It became obvious that many leaders don't need imagination and that it might actually get in the way.**

I first noticed many years' ago that classical creativity is often missing in leaders. I puzzled, 'how can leaders cope without it?' Then, it became obvious that many leaders don't need imagination and that it might actually get in the way. This led me to conclude that, interestingly, imagination or creativity is not a necessary skill for leaders. Why? Because they usually have more than enough bright younger managers in their most imaginative and vigorous phases of development. That is when imagination and creativity are at their most virile. Imagination is (usually) a trait associated with youth. It nearly always dies down in later life (almost all the great scientific innovators make their Nobel Prize level breakthroughs in the third decade of life, long before most leaders get to the top). Furthermore, being

> **Leaders don't need ideas. High-quality judgement is a much more desirable quality.**

the originator of one idea can actually get in the way of the ability to decide which is the best from among several contrasting solutions to a problem. It is remarkable how few leaders or senior managers have the creative plant skill, as defined by Belbin. To summarize, the key reasons why imagination is not a necessary prerequisite to leadership are:

- imaginative skills tend to be associated with passion while leadership requires dispassion and objective judgement to choose the best idea. You cannot do that if one of the many ideas is your own;
- very few people have imagination and leaders cannot be disqualified because they lack it;
- compared to even the few people with imagination there are even fewer good leaders with high quality judgement.

Thus imagination is unnecessary in a leader. They have to know how to exploit the imaginative ideas of others, to turn them into wealth for their corporation. Consider the case study below. It demonstrates one of the sources of my belief that leaders don't need ideas. High-quality judgement is a much more desirable quality.

Case study 6.2

'NO IDEAS' IS GOOD

One of the saddest aspects of the high-quality leadership career of Sir Peter Thompson was his resignation. He resigned at the age of 60 from his chairmanship of the National Freight Consortium. He was a very youthful 60-year-old with a young wife and two young children below the age of ten at the time. The company went downhill after he left.

Over dinner, some years later, I asked why he had resigned prematurely, as I saw it. He replied, 'Well, Cyril, I had run out of fresh ideas. I thought that if I didn't have any ideas of my own for the business, I had a duty to move out of the way and let somebody else do the job.'

I then realized what a terrible mistake that had been. Once he had no new ideas he would make an even better leader than before (and he was formidably good before!). He could then concentrate on dispassionately using his best judgement to select which of the many ideas his young executives were putting forward was truly the best. There was far less chance of a mistake when none of the ideas he had to choose from belonged to him.

Interestingly, entrepreneurs are also often surprisingly unimaginative, even dull, because they need very few original ideas to make lots of profits. Indeed, too many ideas can get in the way. Great entrepreneurs usually make their fortunes by implementing a few good ideas ruthlessly, brilliantly, and repetitiously, with quality. Consider, for example, Bill Gates at MicroSoft. He has built the world's biggest fortune on one idea and one product, ruthlessly exploited and implemented. Unusually, Richard Branson has had more ideas – but the same comment of single-minded exploitation of the few ideas applies.

Another trait that one seldom observes in leaders is a passionate need to know. That trait appears to be superfluous. Perhaps it's because data bombards the leader all the time, particularly with regard to people and their personal problems. Often they don't have time to deal with all these problems, which actually get in the way of the leader's real work. This does not contradict earlier advice where I said that both people and ethics are important (especially when reducing the numbers of people in the organization). This is different. The leader cannot get involved in excessive detail about individuals. This won't stop them focusing on those individuals who are essential to the excellence of the leader's own performance. Leaders don't need detail and they usually do not seek out data. One must hypothesize that they rely on receiving so much information that they will get all they need to know when they want to take any necessary decisions.

I have also noticed that leaders don't need to be good at detail, especially finishing and checking. Again, this is explained because these personal skills become increasingly unnecessary as they move up the corporate ladder and accumulate people around them to do the finishing and checking for them. It is more important to exploit their immense ability to create wealth than to make them finish off detail and dot i's and cross t's.

When Cable and Wireless plc, a leading UK based international telecommunications and cable entertainment business, was attempting a cultural revolution in its subsidiary, Mercury Communications, in the early 1990s they dismissed many higher level managers' and executives' secretaries or personal assistants, saying that they expected their managers to use modern technology to manage their own office. This created the astonishing phenomenon of managers on salaries of up to £100 000 per annum doing their own typing, when that work could have been more effectively accomplished in half the time by secretaries who could be hired at 15 per cent of the price of an executive! Cable and Wireless eventually got itself into quite a mess. By abolishing secretarial support people's capacity to be effective at what they were paid to do was reduced. It was their executive work that suffered.

Characteristics leaders should not have

Anger is one characteristic that leaders should either not start with or should certainly lose before they get to any position of influence or power. Besides the fact that anger is a useless emotion that achieves little, it certainly gets in the way of dispassionate and objective judgement. Furthermore, a display of anger tends to intimidate and frighten people, lessening their courage, neutralizing their

Anger only gets in the way.

imagination and distorting their ability to think straight. Leaders always need to remember that their title and office exude a great deal of power in their subordinates' eyes. Their interests are better served by staying calm and trying to remove the effects of power and status to get the best out of people. Anger only gets in the way. The same applies to all excessive emotionality which causes tension and creates strain for everybody in and around the business.

It is probably vital that a leader should not suffer from *indecisiveness*. Although this is primarily a characteristic of nominal leaders, it can do immense damage when executives suffer from an indecisive leader. Sometimes it manifests itself in an inability to stop collecting data before taking decisions – sometimes called 'analysis paralysis'. I remember meeting a board director at an international engineering business. This delightful and pleasant 'nominal leader' was reputed not to have taken a single decision since he had been appointed to the board role. His MBA had given him immense skills in manipulating data, which he could never stop collecting. Meanwhile, all the best executives had left his division in frustration. His desk and office were piled high with paper, reports and requests for action authorization from his people in the field. The worst cases had been on his desk for two years or more. His business, eventually, went down the tubes and was later taken over by a larger engineering business, at a relatively low stock price.

Leaders are also better fitted to do their job if they have no irrational prejudices and are open to the maximum number of relevant inputs from any source. It also helps if the leader does not need to be seen as a dominant personality. Any lack of personal balance or equilibrium not only makes it harder for them to take balanced judgements but also destabilizes the people who work for them. Nominal leaders can be obsessive about detail. Strategic leaders do not see the need to obsess about detail. They consider it a waste of time, because there are usually people around to deal with detail. Excessive attention to detail removes the quality leader's capacity to focus on the big picture and make judgements about the large strategic issues. I find it terrifying that I have had to attend many board meetings of £multi-billion revenue businesses and hear endless discussions about car policies or, worse, debates about minute quantities of expenditure, while investments worth many millions go through 'on the nod'.

What skills and characteristics are essential?

Great leaders require a capacity to make quality decisions using judgement about complex sets of data. They have to combine this with an insight into the human psyche because their thinking and decision making must be implemented by people. Leaders need to be able to predict the future accurately and to intuit what their customers will want and what they will be able to afford. They have to be able to persuade their stakeholders that their decisions are right. They have to believe in their own decisions in order to persuade anybody else to want to implement them. They will need moral fibre and backbone to see it through, because they will need to continue to believe in their policies, long after others have decided their ideas were not really so bright, after all!

Leaders must be clever enough to command the respect of the greatest brains in their organization. But they must also retain enough appearance of 'ordinariness' to be able to communicate well with any employee at any level in the organization. They need the empathy of a saint while retaining the ability to be cold-hearted and totally dispassionate when deciding the best objective course for the future of the organization. They need the ability to present, visually and verbally, at every level of stakeholders' motley abilities to listen and see and understand. They must be both ordinary and extraordinary. They must be both clever and wise. Above all, they must be capable of inspiring their followers, with that special ability to create in their employees the desire to do the leader's bidding and fulfil their vision for the organization.

It's a formidable list of qualities!

What kind of brain does a leader need?

I am distinguishing the idea of intellectual qualities here from the other qualities we have discussed, such as traits and character. This section refers to the quality of what the leader is born with. In other words, it goes to the heart of the title of this book. I believe the key intellectual characteristics of the best leaders I have observed work in a series of balanced paradoxes. Their brain works differently to others and seems to use a range of motors, exercises and spectra to arrive at conclusions. Let's describe the range. They are both fast and slow, depending whether they wish to grind data or arrive at conclusions. They can approach problems with a heavy-duty grinding machine, yet become swiftly decisive with a light touch when the moment of decision is right. They are both darting and accurate in their honing in on relevant data. They can be simultaneously questioning and decisive, while still communicating clearly to their subordinates. At other times, I have observed the same leaders being ponderous while still capable of lateral thinking. I have seen their accurate but general search for knowledge and information, sifting many contradictory inputs. Then their mind swoops and incisively poses the relevant question which, without losing the accuracy of the rifle, invites a blunderbuss of information. This may then be used to generate the general policy which will facilitate the exploitation of valuable markets which previously were hidden from all concerned.

I have watched these individuals with their unceasing mental energy exploiting their high-quality subconscious skills (the very best thinking is often done by these people while asleep). Then they look at problems whose answers are impossible to fathom. They work their brain and come to conclusions that are obviously right when they have made up their mind.

ENTREPRENEURIALISM VS. CORPORATISM

Most entrepreneurs are not inventive but are organizational and determined. Leaders have to fit their particular skills into the types of organization available. Entrepreneurs, by and large, are not usually employable

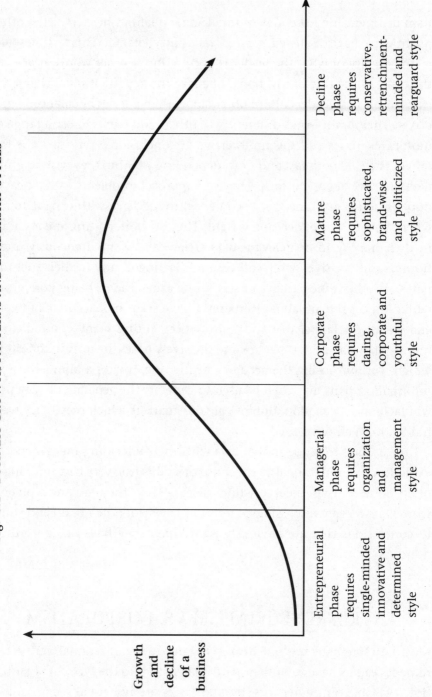

Fig. 6.1 BUSINESS GROWTH PATTERNS AND LEADERSHIP STYLES

Growth and decline of a business

Entrepreneurial phase requires single-minded innovative and determined style

Managerial phase requires organization and management style

Corporate phase requires daring, corporate and youthful style

Mature phase requires sophisticated, brand-wise and politicized style

Decline phase requires conservative, retrenchment-minded and rearguard style within the corporate context. Organizations have life cycles. They are conceived and born, usually with the aid of an entrepreneur. Then they grow, often still led by the entrepreneur but with the assistance of professional managers. Eventually the organization becomes 'corporate', gets floated on a stock market and its shares are distributed among many owners.

Every stage described above needs a special form of leadership. It is up to the leaders to decide what form is best suited to their skill range and aptitudes.

Consider the strange example of the construction and exploitation of the Channel Tunnel. This massive project, which never had much chance of being commercially viable, needed a very special type of corporate entrepreneur. They found their man in Sir Alastair Morton. He was exactly the right type of tough, corporate, jungle warrior to carry out such a huge project. He battled with governments, bankers (a bountiful number), two competitive nationalities (French and British) and finally competition from the likes of P & O, the largest ferry company having an interest in the Channel Tunnel's failure. Sir Alastair had to retain his fiercest qualities and aggression to complete his task. More gentle behaviour would have been inappropriate. A less fierce person would not have made it. It took his eternally, driven spirit and compulsion to complete the task of building the Tunnel itself.

THE EVOLUTION OF BUSINESSES

The first phase of an organization's life requires entrepreneurial leadership. This is individualistic and quite different from the type of classical organizational leadership dealt with in this book. What are the key characteristics required in this phase? What is different? The entrepreneur needs to be innovative (at least about one idea). They need a flexible concept of morality (while not being immoral, they need to see fairness differently from the way the general public understands morality and fairness). They have to be highly persistent and able to cope with setbacks, with a passion and dogmatism about being right. It helps to be inspirational as a leader to get any followers at all; also, they probably need to be highly innovative and creative. Entrepreneurs make rules for themselves, They don't accept society's rules.

During the next phase some managerial and some corporate behaviour becomes necessary. The organization grows and needs human resource policies. Its market share becomes established and needs to be consolidated with management policies and market dexterity. It needs to develop barriers to entry against new competition by persuading politicians to provide rules for safety and other necessary standards to protect the public and their customers. It requires a classical manager, rather than the single-minded entrepreneur. This is the time in the history of many entrepreneurially started businesses that typical classical fights break out between the founding father and the corporate investors. Examples here are the battle between Steve Jobs, founder of Apple Computers and his own executive appointee; or between Alan Sugar, founder of Amstrad, an electronics business, and the shareholders who would not allow him to take his business private and refused his takeover bid. In spite of his own views, Sugar had to make them and himself richer by staying locked into a public company!

HOW LEADERS MOVE IDEAS FROM CREATIVITY TO EXECUTIVE IMPLEMENTATION

There appears, in most businesses of any size, to be a fairly predictable pattern of action. It normally goes in three stages:

Stage 1   In normal corporations, ideas come from the Research & Development or New Product Development departments.

Stage 2   Move from there into marketing for analysis of potential sales and their sustainability.

Stage 3   From there into operational analysis and thence production.

What should the leader be doing at each of these stages?

Stage 1   Ensure corporation is making appropriate level of investment in R&D and NPD.

Stage 2   Ensure organization is marketing-oriented and that marketing is keenly monitoring and stands ready to grab best ideas almost before they are ready.

Stage 3   Ensure that operations care about the success of products and use their knowledge of practical market and consumer usage considerations to enhance the eventual market product.

AT&T offers an interesting insight which is fairly typical of the telecommunications industry. Traditionally, they have had a research centre continuously preparing ideas which nobody has tested against criteria such as, 'will anybody out there be interested in this concept or product if it ever gets to the market?' While the business remains so profitable they need only a small percentage of their ideas to become successful to justify their existence. As soon as AT&T has a downturn in its performance, one must anticipate the research department being among the first to be cut back, to force them to be more selective about what they choose to research and develop.

ICI displayed similar characteristics before the chairman, Sir John Harvey-Jones, forced the research people to justify their existence with prognostications about the market for their research. If they couldn't demonstrate a profitable market he made them stop spending the money.

While the above-described stages are taking place, the leader must keep the overall portfolio of company products and services within his sights. He must also simultaneously consider a whole range of other options:

- the average age of the product and services portfolio
- whether the balance of products is in primary, secondary or final (mature) stages of their product life cycle
- whether the general portfolios of the organization are becoming obsolete
- whether the organization should be moving strategically into newer areas of investment and development which offer greater capacity for long-term survival and succour to the body of the organization
- which combination of exploitation of the mature portfolio and investment in new development will keep the balance of the stakeholders in equilibrium.

It's a fairly formidable list. It probably enforces the concept that leaders without creativity are as useful as cars without fuel or people without food.

SUMMARY

This chapter has debated the concept that leadership creativity is fundamentally different from that of the generally acknowledged inventiveness of normal managers and strategic thinkers. It has described the creative balances and qualities that leaders need, as well as the traits and skills they ought to acquire. It also sets out qualities they do not require. It closes with a layout of the different styles and skills that leaders may need at different stages in the evolution of particular businesses. It should not be expected that any one leader will have all the styles. The implications of the argument are that businesses should change their leaders as the needs of the business change. It may be more efficacious than expecting the leader to manage the total gamut of styles.

> **Leadership creativity is fundamentally different from that of the generally acknowledged inventiveness of normal managers and strategic thinkers.**

RECOMMENDED READING FOR CHAPTER 6

Adair, J. (1988) *Effective Leadership*. London: Pan.

Axtell, R. E. (1991) *Gestures*. Chichester: John Wiley & Sons.

Belbin, R. M. (1991) *Management Teams*. Oxford: Butterworth Heinemann.

Belbin, M. (1993) *Team Roles at Work*. Oxford: Butterworth Heinemann.

Berne, E. (1968) *Games People Play*. Harmondsworth: Penguin.

Briggs-Myers, I. (1992) *Gifts Differing*. Palo Alto, CA: Consulting Psychologists Press.

Chapman, E. N. (1977) *Your Attitude is Showing*. Palo Alto, CA: Science Research Associates.

Covey, S. R. (1989) *The 7 Habits of Highly Effective People*. New York: Simon & Schuster.

Crainer, S. (1996) *Key Management Ideas*. London: Pitman Publishing.

Ferrucci, P. (1990) *What We May Be*. London: Aquarian/Thorsons.

Goleman, D. (1996) *Emotional Intelligence*. London: Bloomsbury.

Harris, T. A. (1973) *I'm OK – You're OK*. London: Pan.

Kiersey, D. and Bates, M. (1984) *Please Understand Me*. Del Mar, CA: Prometheus Nemesis Book Company.

Lewis, R. and Lowe, P. (1992) *Individual Excellence*. London: Kogan Page.

McClelland, D. (1961) *The Achieving Society*. Princeton, NJ: Van Nostrand.

McGregor, D. (1960) *The Human Side of Enterprise*. New York: McGraw-Hill.

Peter, L. J. and Hull, R. (1979) *The Peter Principle*. London: Pan.

Peters, T. J. and Waterman, R. H., Jr. (1982) *In Search of Excellence*. New York: Harper & Row.

Biographies of companies and leaders

Bayer, T. (1991) *Maxwell: The Outsider*. London: Mandarin.

Bramson, A. (1990) *Pure Luck*. Wellingborough: Patrick Stephens.

Love, J. F. (1995) *McDonald's: Behind the Arches*. New York: Bantam.

Malik, R. (1975) *And Tomorrow the World?* London: Millington.

Maney, K. (1995) *Megamedia Shakeout*. New York: John Wiley.

Morita, A. (1994) *Made in Japan*. London: HarperCollins.

Shawcross, W. (1992) *Murdoch*. London: Chatto & Windus.

Thompson, P. (1990) *Sharing the Success*. London: Fontana.

Vanderbilt, A., II (n.d.) *Fortune's Children*. Falmouth: Sphere.

Walton, S. (1993) *Made in America*. New York: Bantam.

THE POLITICS OF LEADERSHIP ROLES

....

This chapter examines the nature of politics in organizational life. It questions the degree to which leaders have to be skilled at politics and analyzes whether they need political skills as a process or a way of life.

....

ONE MAN'S POLITICS ...

Politics at the top of organizations is that part of organizational decision making which eases the process of getting things done. This is neither a trivial nor trite statement. It could sound like it to those who 'can't stand politics', or imagine that politics at the top of organizations are internecine and nasty and that all board rooms are a dens of vipers and fit only for the *mafiosi* of corporate ambition. In fact, life at the top of almost all the organizations I have been close to is pleasant, most of the time. I am sure that this will ring eminently true for those leaders who know how to get

What appears to be politics is, mostly, *process*.

things done. Most board rooms are free of the unpleasant politics that are portrayed in television dramas or falsely rehearsed in Sunday newspapers by journalists when they are short on information and long on imagination. Naturally there are times when the temperature rises and leaders need to summon all their concentration, guile and cunning to deal with crises of people or process. But those moments are relatively ephemeral and pass quickly. The general ambiance is quiet and, when led by quality leaders, emits a quiet hum of 'making things happen'.

What appears to be politics is, mostly, *process*. It is the way that leaders persuade the stakeholders to consent to and approve their vision. There is an etiquette of senior echelon work that needs to be understood by anybody seriously wishing to play in the top league in industry. It is well-mannered and relatively straightforward. But it has to be done right. If it isn't, the other parties become suspicious and assume there may be dangers lurking. Part of the etiquette requires the leader to know what to do and how to do it, without actually having it explained in so many words. This is not because it's all some code learned at public or business schools, but because nobody is totally sure, all the time, of quite what one is supposed to do or when. Let me give an example.

Case study 7.1

GETTING THE PROCESS RIGHT

The chairman of a large engineering business had been misled into taking a non-executive appointment after an illustrious career in the City, on the basis that it would be practically a semi-retirement. Unfortunately, it did not turn out like that. Shortly after he was appointed he had to find, within a month or two, a new finance director. Within weeks of starting work, the new FD came to the chairman to tell him that the CEO appeared to be materially exploiting his position somewhat ruthlessly. The CEO was ordering hundreds of bottles of wine a month for his personal cellar but charging it to the company. Furthermore, he appeared to be keeping, at the company's expense, an apartment in New York and another in Australia. He also appeared to have a mistress installed in each country. Both mistresses were on the company payroll at inflated salaries but did not seem to be reporting for work, at least, not at the office. What should the FD do?

For this highly ethical chairman there could be no doubt. The CEO had to go and the sooner the better. But the FD had told him in confidence. And the FD was really a subordinate of the CEO, and should not, in fact, have been speaking to the chairman at all. The chairman also had to take account of the fact that this CEO had grown the business 500 per cent in five years and deserved better than an ignominious end to his career. Anyway, it could damage the share price, which was languishing at that time, and make the company a takeover target at a time when it would be in no position to defend itself, without an effective CEO.

The chairman spent the next few months selecting new non-executive directors who were his personal appointees to the board. He then spoke to each privately, once they were installed, and told them of the problem. They agreed to authorize him to offer the CEO a package that would pay him off, on condition he went immediately. It set conditions of mutual secrecy. He then asked the CEO to resign with immediate effect, which he did. The episode was over.

But it had taken six months, and many more bottles of wine and wages to mistresses than most leaders would like.

That is a typical 'political' story from a board room. It would never normally see the light of day. Even now, of course, no names are being revealed. All the players have long since retired from the field of battle. But it is a true story. Can such episodes ever be stopped? The simple answer is 'no'. Can the process whereby removal takes less time be improved? Again, probably not. There is some merit in the etiquette of the board room. If it became too simple to organize removals, there would be many more false accusations and precipitate dismissals. It would begin to resemble the stories on the television rather than the rare event it tends to be, in the real world.

The politics at senior levels in organizations vary by organization. It tends to be a function of the culture of each business which, in turn, tends to be correlated to the nature and preferences of the leaders themselves. The amount of politics, as 'corporate etiquette', is also a direct function of the size of the organization. The larger the business, the more likely the board is to contain members of the 'great and good' and other people who have spent lifetimes developing their career and their reputation. These people are usually reluctant to get themselves and their good names caught up in unnecessary melodrama or unpleasant newspaper headlines, if a matter can be dealt with without these disturbances. At the same time, they are highly sensitive to any danger to their investment in building their personal reputation over a lifetime career.

The politics of process, the normal way things are done at top levels, is relatively benign. It usually requires the leader to spend time removing psychological and other obstacles that might prevent the board from approving the leader's proposals. The purpose is always to neutralize the power of those who are able to stop any decision being taken, unless they have good business and strategic reasons for doing so, and to ensure that those who approve do so vigorously. In other words, the leader spends time, as would any member of any church committee or member of the local school governors, organizing all the human and other resources to agree a 'yes' at the appropriate formal meeting (normally a board).

WHY CALL IT POLITICS?

We call these matters 'politics' for want of a better word. Politics is really just another name for organizational process. Unfortunately, the word is often used pejoratively by those who do not know how to cope with the process or who cannot learn the etiquette of the politics at senior level in the organization. I often conclude that, when an executive says he is 'tired of the politics of his job' or 'I wouldn't want the job above this present one because of all the politics', he is really saying that he does not have the competence to move to the next level. At every level, politics is just the process by which one gets things done. Another mistake that is sometimes made is to believe that when all the top people are being mutually pleasant and nice to each other, it is just the bosses scratching each others' backs

> **When an executive says he is 'tired of the politics of his job' or 'I wouldn't want the job above this present one because of all the politics', he is really saying that he does not have the competence to move to the next level.**

and 'playing politics'. Frequently, being nice to each other and being political are just happy coincidences. Take, for example, some work I was asked to do with a divisional MD who also sat on the board of his group business. The job was, ostensibly, to help him prepare a strategy review for the group board. He had never done one before and needed help. He had read my book on strategy analysis (Levicki 1996) and thought I could understand. In fact the job was less about preparing strategy and more about helping this maturing business-man to become less naïve about the politics of the board room. The review was really a means for his group chairman to transfer attention from the under performance of the group (that the owners of the business were beginning to notice). Meanwhile, the division led by my client was doing well but its results were being distorted by unjustified property charges, being made by the group FD against the division, following the instructions of the group chairman. We decided not to call the group chairman's unfairness to book. Instead we offered to make a private presentation to each of the members of the board (especially the non-executive directors) prior to the main board meeting when the strategy was due to be presented. At these private presentations we ensured that they understood how well the business was really doing if only the property were to be charged properly and fairly. At the review itself, all the MD's ideas were accepted. They even voted several million £s of extra capital to sort out the apparent property problems! The Group Chairman forgot to minute this particular item ... so the board was reminded at the next meeting and the group chair grudgingly had to rewrite the minutes and hand over the money! Was this politics or just the way you do things at board level?

Politics can be bad rather than good process

If managing the process to achieve the necessary strategic intent and good effect is a part (and a good one) of the leader's range of skills, when are politics bad? They may be considered to be wrongly used when they are employed not to implement the decision-making process but, rather, to achieve petty or personal goals. In the example given above, there are some who might suggest that politics were being played. The actions of the Group Chairman should have been denounced outright and his bluff called. But why would the MD want to do that? The chairman had actually done a fine job for the business, for over a decade. If the owners were to decide that his useful period in office was finished, they should make up their own minds and do something about it. That was not the divisional leader's remit and it would have been invidious to interfere or try in any way to poison the minds of the rest of the board against the chairman. The main objective was to ensure that his division received fair treatment.

Most managers start to use politics in the worst sense when they are being overwhelmed by their task and are not up to it. I remember working with an executive who had been promoted to the board of a £2 billion revenue business, at the tender age of 38. He had an appalling record of achievement. Every business he had supposedly enhanced, disintegrated as soon as he left the post. But he always managed to blame it on his successor. He had done only three leadership jobs, running rather small businesses with of revenues between £22m and £95m. When he was promoted to the board, he was also put in charge of a business with revenues, at the start, of £750m. He liked to describe himself as a 'turn-round specialist'. I realized later, that what he meant was that, because he got all his businesses into trouble, he then had to turn them around! But nobody could understand how the chairman, HR director and the rest of the directors could not see through this man's incompetence and realize he brought no business skills to the board. Furthermore, he was likely to ruin the best division in the business, which they had given to him to run. In fact that is what happened. Under this man's leadership the best division became the worst within three years. The share price of the business collapsed and a new chairman and CEO were appointed. Most fascinating of all, this individual was the only member of the previous board directors to survive the new regime. Every other director was sacked. He survived a further two years before they realized he had no idea about running a business or delivering quality results. The whole saga was a testament to the one skill this man had – the highest level of political skill I have ever witnessed. It was composed of a subtle ability to flatter his bosses and never offend his peer group. He retired, a relatively rich man, at the age of 48. They found him out in the end.

At the end of the day, there will always be some managers who are more skilled than average at getting on with people. This does not indicate whether they do or do not have any leadership ability. But when they have this human quality of being nice to everybody around and never ruffling feathers, they will certainly be able to maximize the use of any leadership skills they do have. Like the individual I described above, they can create a career from their 'political' or 'human' skills. Again, if that is all they have, who can blame them for exploiting their assets. It is the organization's job to ensure that people are effective rather than merely 'nice'. Niceness is a pleasant bonus, when it is available.

Unfortunately, wrong-minded nominal leaders will always be using some sort of politics to get their way against the wishes or good of the organization. It is important that good leaders ensure that political processes are kept to a minimum and used only for the good of the organization.

The politics of the board of directors

Boards of directors exist to give guidance and direction to the leader and to act as a final buffer against wrong decision making by the leader. This is, of course, a contradiction, because it is difficult to serve both purposes at once. If you are there to help, it is difficult to retain a critical and appraising eye on what the leader is doing. On the other hand, if you retain only a critical eye on everything the leader does, it won't be long before you find some, or many, faults. That is just the nature of searching for things going wrong in any human endeavour – you can always find fault!

The board also exists to manage change, when the leadership of the firm proves inadequate. We have discussed elsewhere in this book that this is a function they find very hard to implement. It is nearly always the case that the situation has to be really dire before the board manages to assemble the necessary power to do something about a deep-seated and important problem. Often, by that time, it is too late to do anything constructive about the problem. Profoundly difficult strategic quandaries in an organization often have to start with a change of the leadership that created the problems. Unfortunately, by the time the board summons up the courage and means to resolve the problem in such a radical way, it will have become extremely difficult for the successor to put things right.

The board also exists to legally represent the owners' and the shareholders' interests. This applies whether there is direct representative of the owners or shareholders on the board or not.

THE VARIABLES OF POLITICS

If we can agree to use the word 'politics' without pejorative overtones, let's consider the variables which govern the quantity of politics to be found in the average board of directors. They are set out in Table 7.1.

Let's examine each of the variables in turn.

Table 7.1 The variables of organizational politics

The political variable	Comment	Importance and frequency
The size of the business	The arithmetic is the most compelling factor in politics in organizations (see Gibrat 1931)	< 100 should be non-existent > 100 but < 1000 very low levels > 1000 but < 10k managerial levels skills required – it's small but can be dirty > 10k but < 50k understanding sophisticated process beginning to be important, occupies 25% of time > 50k but < 100k Subtle understanding, sharp instincts and capacity to pro-actively cope when being attacked are vital > 100k You cannot get to this level if you don't understand and know how to cope with every subtlety of organizational politics
The number of persons who appoint people to membership	Different boards are nominated in various ways. Some have many people with nominating power; others few or one.	The more people who have the right to nominate or appoint, the less unified the board and the greater the politics. The fewer people nominating or appointing, the greater the unity and the lesser the politics.
If the leader does the nominating	The leader is usually, in this instance, the chair. Can be problematic if the chair and CEO fall out	If only one nominator or appointing person, the least politics but the greater the danger of the board being railroaded. Can be useful in decreasing boardroom dissent
The befriending skills of the leader	These work in both finding good board members and maintaining relationships with them	Because befriending is a key leadership skill, this can usually be assumed. It is therefore not a key factor, but, nevertheless, important.
The quality of the leader	See above	There are not many quality leaders, so this is a frequent cause of problems. In my personal work with leaders, I spend more time on helping them cope with the politics while they learn to become a quality leader than on anything else.
The quantity and quality of meetings prior to the board meeting	This tends to be a factor of precedent and culture	The dining habit tends to take place in those boards which meet less frequently. Normally, this is an indicator of less political intervention from the board. Usually one can assume that the more frequent the board meetings, the more politics there will be.
The competence of the leader	A leader's best skills should not be in politics, but it helps if they have them	Competence in a leader is a function of their total leadership skills. However, in general, the more competent the leader in their strategic duties and ability to make profits, the less politics they will need to do

Fig. 7.1 SUPPING AT THE BOARD TABLE: A CLASSIC SCENARIO

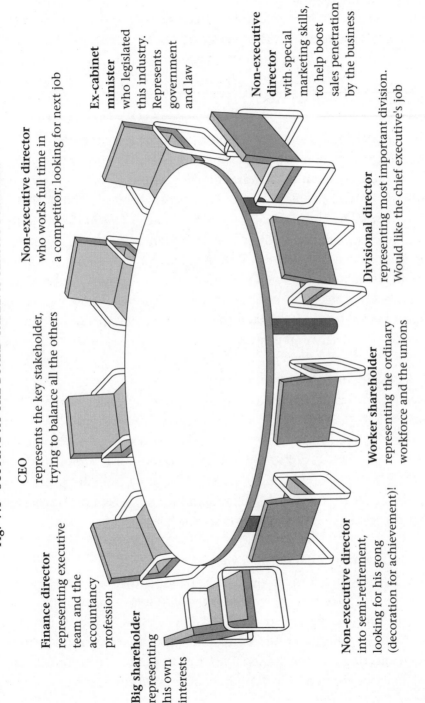

Finance director
representing executive
team and the
accountancy
profession

Big shareholder
representing
his own
interests

Non-executive director
into semi-retirement,
looking for his gong
(decoration for achievement)!

CEO
represents the key stakeholder,
trying to balance all the others

Non-executive director
who works full time in
a competitor; looking for next job

**Ex-cabinet
minister**
who legislated
this industry.
Represents
government
and law

**Non-executive
director**
with special
marketing skills,
to help boost
sales penetration
by the business

Divisional director
representing most important division.
Would like the chief executive's job

Worker shareholder
representing the ordinary
workforce and the unions

The size of the business

It appears to be an absolute that the larger the organization, emphatically, the more the politics. This is a consequence of the decisions tending to be larger in magnitude, also, and the greater the number of more complex barriers they have to pass through. Large organizations need, and tend to have, more filtering systems.

The number of persons who appoint people to membership

The more people nominating or appointing people to membership of the board, the more politics. This is a function of the probability that when only one or two people have nominated people to the board, they are likely to have had unitary ideas about the strategic reasons for their nominations or appointments. They may have wanted to beef up the marketing skills, or consolidate the auditing skills, or control top salaries by assembling a better remuneration committee. A diminishing variable on this rule is that the longer the period since people were appointed, the less united the board and the greater the politics, because the unifying vision will have receded over the years.

If the leader does the nominating

Usually, with good leaders, if they nominate people there is less politics. Obviously, if a leader is stupid enough to nominate people who were unlikely to vote with their ideas, by and large, they are too foolish to be a good leader. This is not to say a great leader will just nominate a set of toadies. Rather, it is asserting that a good leader will appoint people who, while capable of vigorous debate, will, in the end, agree on a single vision with the leader about the direction for the business.

The befriending skills of the leader

Generally, the better the leader is at befriending the non-executive directors, the less politics there will be. This will result from the leader ensuring that they receive explanations about policies, in private, before board meetings, in order to ensure unity and approval, in advance, of formal board meetings. If the leader finds the board members unwilling or unhappy about any proposals, they would be well advised to change them before bringing them before the board. When they have been changed, they should be checked again, to see if they meet with approval. Boards are not meant to be rubber stamps, but neither are they the best place to sort out problems.

> Surprises in strategic proposals or the business results represent the contrary of good management, because it means that the managers are not anticipating events, and acting with prescience, in advance of difficulties.

The quality of the leader

Usually, the better the leader the less politics, because great leaders never present surprises to their board. Surprises both shock and worry other board members, particularly the non-executive directors. They usually, see their function as ensuring the smooth management of the business and guaranteeing that the executive managers and leaders carry out their responsibilities properly. Surprises in strategic proposals or the business results represent the contrary of good management, because it means that the managers are not anticipating events, and acting with prescience, in advance of difficulties. That is poor leadership and needs to be scrutinized carefully.

The quantity and quality of meetings prior to the board meeting

If there is an established habit of holding meetings prior to the actual board meeting, it usually indicates that problems and objections are being looked for and solved before the meeting itself. This is usually different to the pre-board dinner or elaborate lunch that some boards indulge in. Those are far less useful, and sometimes positively dangerous for the health of the older directors! But, in essence, all good leaders ensure that they are going to get a 'yes' to anything they are going to present to the board, well before the actual meeting itself. If there is a chance of the board voting against a policy the leader is advocating, good leaders just don't present it, for the excellent reason that they would never want their board to develop the habit of saying 'No'. Once they have learned to do so, there is always the danger they will continue to do so. Better never to let them get the taste of blood! A sensible CEO or chairperson would always find out what it would take, in terms of changing their intended presentation and content, to adapt it to the requirements of the board. Even then, they would test it again with the members who have raised the previous objections, before the next board meeting, to ensure that they can expect a favourable reaction, the next time they present it.

Some readers may be thinking that this surely means that board meetings are a charade, a rigmarole of procedure with no substance. That is not true. In most businesses, the board can represent the best thinking powers within the whole organization. Indeed, in some, vigorous debates do take place at the actual board meetings. I am suggesting, from my experience, however, that this is not the best place for the really hard and rough debates to take place. Such debates and arguments are best conducted prior to, and outside, formal board meetings, since these meetings are not the best forum in which to improve the quality of the decision. At best, the board should conduct discussions to ensure that no key points have been missed in the preparation for the decision. If the process of debate, rather than discussion, takes over at the board meeting, the arguments tend to go with the people who are better at debating, rather than those who have the best ideas. Often the truly innovative and insightful business people on the board are less articulate than the tough debaters. They may lose the debate, but the business will lose their good ideas!

> If the process of debate, rather than discussion, takes over at the board meeting, the arguments tend to go with the people who are better at debating, rather than those who have the best ideas.

One old campaigner I knew, an ex-academic who later worked in politics as a 'thinker' for a prime minister, was highly skilled at political debate, although less than useful at anything to do with business. He'd never truly experienced commercial life. His influence on many boards was highly unbalanced because his debating skills were as excellent as his business knowledge was absent. He caused inordinate and pointless disruption on many boards where he sat. Unfortunately, his prestige and his title kept him there, even when many board members had realized he added no value at all.

Competent leaders dominate their boards. It is part of their skill set. Of course, if it is the only skill they have the business is in trouble, because a poor but politically adept leader will be able to persuade the board to allow them to retain their leadership position, long after any quality board would have discovered their incompetence. This is the type of situation where it helps when other City institutions, such as pension funds managers or bankers, exercise their influence and intervene when they become dissatisfied with the leadership and the business results it is delivering.

Similarly, because good leaders dominate their boards through their personality, they should never receive surprises from their board. If they are using their befriending skills, they should know what's going on in the mind of the individual players on the board, whether executive or non-executive directors. That should enable them to anticipate when trouble looms! A good leader should always, then, be able to exercise their will because they will always have the force of being right. Likewise, they should be able to inspire confidence in the correctness of their decision because they exude leadership competence.

It is sometimes difficult for a strategic leader to organize a change of nominal leader. This applies, for example, in the case of an MD who is the strategic leader of a business, when they have a non-executive chairman, as nominal leader. These nominal leaders are usually little trouble, as long as they realize that they meant to be nominal and are only there in case of emergencies or to act as 'grand regulator' on behalf of the owners, institutions or stock market investors. However, sometimes, they get a taste for interfering and meddling. This can become difficult for the real strategic leader. Life can become somewhat strained in these circumstances. Often the nominal leader becomes a nuisance at the same time that he is also flexing his muscles and trying to capture power. It is probable that he understands power and how to use it if he is in the position of nominal leader, anyway. What should the real leader do? This is when the benefits of maintaining excellent relationships with the other members of the board, particularly the non-executive directors, become most fruitful. It is vital to bring these board members in as allies, either to warn the nominal leader to stop meddling or to help remove him. In all cases it is preferable to instigate the least action possible. Thus, persuading him to back off is better than removing him. Removal is public. He will be induced to fight harder and the organization may be more damaged. Simply getting him back into his box is better both for his self-esteem and for the organization's well-being. Ensuring that he knows what you are doing, and getting him to agree, requires diplomacy and tact of a special nature.

Good leaders know how to do these things. It is probably better if the nominal leader (in the chair position) never even knows that it was the MD who organized the people who finally have the conversation with the chair, over a quiet dinner at a fine restaurant.

One nominal leader I once had the misfortune to work with did the opposite. He was brought in as a nominal leader, with the title 'non-executive chairman', to manage an excellent young MD who was highly rated by the City. However, this cunning and highly political old dog (he had to be because he was useless as a strategic leader) could not cope with the bright young MD, who made him feel as inadequate as he really was. Within months the chairperson had managed to manoeuvre the incumbent MD into resigning. He then replaced him with an idiot who made him feel comparatively intelligent. He then went further and removed the 'non-executive' part of his title. He now runs the corporation as its executive chairman. He is rapidly running the business into massive debt on a growth programme which hasn't the remotest chance of making business profits. Eventually the investors will be forced to take over the company, with terrible losses of their capital and the workers' jobs. The only good news on this particular horizon is that he is now too old to get another job, and so this will be the last organization he ruins.

Case study 7.2

THE BOARD IS THE POWER

I once worked with a leader who had the opposite of the ability to exude confidence and competence. Although his decisions were often strategically correct he was a poor leader, who could never decide how best to inspire his subordinates to adopt his decisions, or keep to one budgetary path. Neither could he convince his board that his strategic ideas had value. After a short time in office, whenever he tried to sell them an idea they would throw it out on principle. Ultimately (using the politics variables described above to analyze what went wrong), he was a poor leader who lacked charisma and character, who had no befriending skills, who failed to inform and get the board's agreement in advance of meetings, and whose board was composed solely of the nominations of his chairman (who had set it up in order to dominate whatever was going on himself).

This poor individual never did get another job when they eventually threw him out.

VISIBLE VS. INVISIBLE POLITICS

If one takes politics to mean, in the broader sense, 'the process employed to get things done at the senior levels of management in the organization', it is sensible to differentiate between visible and invisible politics. The latter means the type of politics I have described above, getting things done smoothly, with pre-board background discussions, ensuring a smooth path for decisions, when they come in front of the board and its sub commit-

> Invisibility in the political process is preferable because it is much more effective than visible politics.

tees for formal processing. These formal processes of the organization will include such meetings as: the remuneration committee; the new products development team; the large projects review board; the finance monitoring subcommittee; and the board's annual review. I contend that, usually, the politics of these systems are best done invisibly, for the reasons stated in the section above. Furthermore, political processes are generally not well viewed by those at lower levels in the organization. Often subordinates may not understand politics and will therefore form a poor impression of those who practise the art within the organization, even when they otherwise think of them as a fine leader.

It is always worth remembering that invisible politics have the advantage of never teaching new tricks to any idiotic old dogs the politics are meant to be dealing with! Furthermore, good leaders, because they are unselfish, sometimes get into situations where they are not being adequately rewarded for their labour. In these circumstances invisible politics are vital in ensuring they get their just rewards. Above all, invisibility in the political process is preferable because it is much more effective than visible politics.

Visible politics can be used consciously by the leader of politics, to demonstrate any principles or any other important values to the general body of the organizations they lead. In these cases the opposite features and values of invisible politics apply. Instead of the principle that it is always better to practise politics invisibly because it gives little or no chance to one's opponents to retaliate or take revenge, the contrary applies. If you are going to use politics visibly to teach a particular lesson to individuals or groups in the organization, then it is best to do full technicolor.

You should only exploit visible politics when the person they are being visibly applied to has no power to retaliate or take their revenge. They have to accept the politics you are applying to them, for the learning purposes of the organization. Examples would be: a public admonition to a manager because he treated an employee rudely or unjustly; an open rejection of a poor budget forecast for next year's achievement, to let the other managers know they must be more ambitious; a public apology in the newspapers for bad service to customers, when this has been demonstrated and the public is angry; public praise for extraordinary performance, to encourage others to try harder.

One would certainly use visible politics to teach an unethical manager a lesson (after trying every other method to change his ways) or to demonstrate to up-and-coming leaders how to actually use politics or processes. One may, on occasion, use them to demonstrate to a recalcitrant board that it is wrong-minded and must change its attitude. Occasionally one simply needs to remove a fool from the scene and visible politics is the only way.

To summarize: always remember that invisible beats visible politics and that the less frequent the use of visible politics, the more powerful it is as a teaching device.

Other occasions when good leaders use politics to further their careers

A leader may arrive in a post to find themselves saddled with a particularly unappreciative board. To demonstrate their own effectiveness to the board, and to begin the process of mastery, they may need to use the art of politics to allow the board to understand better how matters will be conducted in the future. Sometimes a leader needs to achieve a one-off breakthrough in strategy. This is a way to demonstrate or convince the board that the leader is on the right path. Such times call for the powerful use of every political trick the leader can summon up.

There are other times, such as when one's career is at a fulcrum of change. These may be occasions when the leader has achieved a breakthrough in terms of personal skill levels; or has developed their power to conceptualize at a higher level; or, possibly, when their income needs have increased due to family commitments. It may be necessary to demonstrate to the board that they have reached such a point in their career. Under these circumstances, it may sometimes be necessary to exploit political skills to focus the audience's attention onto the situation.

Other occasions when visible politics are appropriate may occur when one has created an winning strategy, or an unbeatable product, or a masterly follow-through to a takeover. The open use of politics may be the best way to intimidate the competition or to announce to the market that you have achieved a winning position!

Stakeholders and the political spider at the centre of the web

I referred to stakeholder theory in Chapter 5. It is worth mentioning that politics and the stakeholder theory are intimately linked. If one regards the leader as the spider at the centre of the web and the stakeholders all around the web, one gets a fairly accurate view of the way many leaders perceive the job they have, as that of managing the stakeholders. The crucial judgement skill of the leader, the spider in the centre of the web, managing the contradictory requirements of all the stakeholders, is both apposite and predictive, especially if one thinks of the tension of the web itself. The stakeholders usually represent most of those with key interests in the business, whether they are large shareholders, founder families, bankers who have made large loans, or eminent members of the industry. The politics of the boardroom are often about managing those stakeholders as members of the board. It can be complex. Consider the following case study.

Case study 7.3

CLASHING CLAIMS CRACK UP CABLE LEADERS

Background to the cable industry in the UK

The UK cable industry was initiated in the 1960's when ITV started as the UK's second channel, delivered mainly by 'Rediffusion'. That business eventually became NTL, a national telephony network. In 1996 it was taken over by CableTel, which adopted its name, and became a UK cable entertainment and telephony business. It is quoted on the US NASDAQ, market although all its interests are in the UK Cable industry.

Most of the other major UK cable businesses are controlled by US cable businesses. Many of these started in the USA because television was always better diffused, with higher quality, by cable rather than by aerial transmitters (the BBC methodology), in the more widely spread and mountainous American cities and states. The UK cable industry is briefly summarised by the following:

Cable & Wireless Communications
6m potential homes/1.5m customers

NTL (including current bid for Comcast)
2.5m potential homes/400k customers

TeleWest Communications
(including current bid for General Cable)
6m potential homes/1.8 m customers

Diamond Cable
1m potential homes/120k customers
ComTel
800k potential homes/100k customers

The largest cable firms in the USA are TCI (1st), Time Warner (2nd), Media One International (3rd) and Cox (4th). TCI has strong interests in making programmes too, although all the major players buy a great deal of product from the leading American network television businesses like NBC and CBS; and from the Hollywood Studios such as Disney, Sony and Fox. The latter is a typical hybrid, however, being controlled by Rupert Murdoch's News International Corporation, which also buys as much as 60 per cent of all the other Hollywood studios' output for transmission outside the USA for its satellite operations' entertainment transmissions around the world. Rupert Murdoch also has a 40 per cent controlling interest in BSkyB in the UK, the main rival to the cable business's entertainment business. BSkyB transmits its programmes by satellite. Murdoch also supplies the cable businesses with the bulk of their programmes for transmission, a strange alliance of supplier and competitor.

TeleWest

TeleWest plc is a quoted UK cable company which has 40 per cent of its shares owned by the public. The rest are owned by international cable firms. TCI (largest in the USA cable industry) and Media One International (third largest in the USA cable industry) have 20.9 per cent each, with an agreement to vote together for majority control (this information is in the public arena). When they cannot agree how to vote, their agreement states they will vote according to the last board policy. Representatives of Cox Cable (third largest cable business in the USA) and SBC (another USA-based cable business) also sit on the board because they each hold 11.4 per cent of the TeleWest shares. Generale des Eaux (a French utility) has 8.5 per cent of the shares (following TeleWest's takeover of General Cable) and also has a guaranteed place on the board. The Chairman of TeleWest is also the President of Media One International.

TCI has strong interests in the supply of entertainment software, which is a key ingredient of the costs of all cable companies. One of its subsidiaries (Flextech), actually supplies a considerable quantity of entertainment programmes to TeleWest. Media One International doesn't yet produce programmes. Its interests stem from a background in telephony in the USA, a totally different business to cable entertainment, although it has grown its cable interests considerably. It does not yet manufacture or supply entertainment software and is a large buyer of programmes in the USA. TCI and Media One International also have different cultures when considering the business. Telephony businesses are traditional, hierarchical, based on standard operating procedures and measure their business on cashflow and minutes of telephony sold. Cable-entertainment businesses are lateral, creative, non-hierarchical and measure themselves on EBITDA, (a measure started in the USA which examines earnings before interest, tax, amortization and depreciation) and the number of viewers.

As a consequence of the different cultures, the types of requests made of the CEO at board meetings, and elsewhere, indicate quite contradictory directions for the business for the CEO to try to enact. Imagine the subtleties required of a CEO of a business like this. He has to bring all major contracts before the board, for approval before signing them. Some relate to deals with the subsidiary of TCI mentioned above, which supplies some of TeleWest's programming. The TeleWest CEO would dearly love to get the board help to apply influence on Sky to write a better contract, which would give him a chance to deliver better results to the shareholders. But some of the stakeholders on the board may have greater economic interests elsewhere. TeleWest is installing new IT systems throughout its business. But the most important customer of the IT supplier is Cox in the USA. The CEO would normally want his board directors to apply their influence on the directors of the IT supply business to ensure he gets better service. But Cox has given a bigger order in the USA to the IT supplier. Naturally, it is hard to get Cox to agree to use the TeleWest's Board influence to get better service.

With a mixture of interests like that, what premium would the reader place upon the CEO's political skills? Interestingly, the business has changed its CEO approximately every 18 months for the first seven years of its existence. It has had a similar burn rate with its chief operating officers. Recently, TeleWest made a bid for General Cable, a business with approximately one million potential homes and an actual 200k customers. It appears that the bid set off further questions about exactly what type of CEO the board wanted to lead the business. The directors of the board decided they were prepared to search for a new CEO. At this point, another CEO decided that was enough – he resigned.

FADS OR TRENDS?

Politics (or the public face of political announcements by leaders) can often be a useful means of signalling by the leader, on behalf of the organization, that the organization is responding to public opinion. This will be applicable in times of media exposure of adverse aspects of a business or industry (e.g., pollution in the oil industry; safety in automobiles). At such a time it is imperative that the public sees that responsible leaders and their businesses both are recognizing and responding to public opinion. The task of deciding what media pressure is merely passing comment and what is profoundly important (reflecting deep-felt public opinion) is dependent upon a combination of the leader's common sense and his intuition. Leaders have to ask themselves the question, 'Is this situation or event a real problem or will it go away unnoticed?' or, 'What type of people are championing the need to take this seriously?' The answers to questions such as these will guide the leader as to what type of action they have to take.

THE TOOL OF SILENCE

The use of silence as a tool is a special skill which many leaders use with tremendous results. Most people have a need to speak, to fill gaps in conversation When there is a silence, they feel psychologically constrained to fill the silence. Most people find it hard to sit in silence when they are in a room with another person. Wise leaders learn to use this awkwardness in the face of silence to good effect. They ask questions about important subjects on which they need information. Often they know that the respondent may not want to give them the information they are seeking. When the other person has given what they hope is a sufficient but not totally honest or full explanation, a judicious use of the tool of silence will often extract, in the end, all the more detailed data and information that is really needed to solve the problem. I have often used silence, both in my research and my work with managers. It is astonishing how much quality information emerges, especially in the last

> The use of silence as a tool is a special skill which many leaders use with tremendous results.

minute or two of any meeting. Of course, when I try it on quality leaders, it just leads to long periods of silence. We're both using the same tool!

The tool of silence is particularly apt for use when there are organizational politics to process. Often, it is wise to not meet trouble half way. In other words, if the leader does not feed speculation, and does not give information where there is no need to do so, the outcome will be facilitated. The judicious use of silence under such circumstances will be immensely useful.

A CLOSING CAUTION

Remember, if you don't use politics, somebody may use politics on you. It is not wise to be a second mover in the political game.

Wise leaders never underestimate politics and its importance. When you hear yourself say, 'I'm fed up with the politics in this organization', it probably indicates you are tired of your career and you have lost control anyway. Remember, if you don't use politics, somebody may use politics on you. It is not wise to be a second mover in the political game. It keeps you on the wrong foot. When you do use politics, you should use them with the absolute minimum of force, and then only when it is vitally necessary. The more politics you use, the less valuable they will be. This will, in turn, reduce the power of any politics you need to use in the future. A good metaphor is to consider politics like the bullets in the barrel of a revolver. Once you have spent the bullets in a battle, you need plenty of time to reload if you are not going to be shot in the heat of battle! If you run out of bullets, you become a sitting duck. Almost all politics are best done secretly (apart from the exceptions listed above). Always ask yourself whether a piece of political behaviour is necessary, or just fun? If the latter, don't do it. As a final reminder, ponder on the lessons of the case study below.

Case study 7.4

DON'T WASTE BULLETS

I described earlier an intelligent CEO who was good at finding correct solutions but terrible at their implementation. There was a time when he was trying to do two important things simultaneously in his business. He wanted to persuade the board to accept a new and revolutionary strategy to save the business from being a potential takeover target. Simultaneously, he needed to get the board to approve the dismissal of one of his divisional directors, who was failing to deliver results. He was advised not to do both at once. The chairman was being 'worked on' by several advisers and the non-executive directors were also being appraised of the need to dismiss this recalcitrant director. They would do the job for the CEO, given a few weeks.

But the CEO could not contain himself. He was utterly fed up with his divisional director. So, against advice, he marched into the chairman's office and demanded his MD's head on a platter. The chairman asked for time to consult the rest of the board. But the CEO insisted. The chairman only gave in once his hand was forced in this way.

Thus the CEO (metaphorically) handed over at least two of the only six bullets he had in his revolver. When the CEO tried to force through his revolutionary strategy at the next board meeting, he was fatally short of bullets. His strategy proposals were turned down. Now he had nowhere to go. He was peremptorily dismissed, three months later.

RECOMMENDED READING FOR CHAPTER 7

Braybrooke, D. and Lindblom, C. D. (1969) *A Strategy of Decision*. Clencoe: Free Press of Clencoe.

Gibrat R., (1931) *Les inégalités économiques*. Paris: Recueil Sirey.

Herder, J. (1992) *The Tao of Leadership*. Aldershot: Gower.

Hickson, D. J. *et al.* (1986) *Top Decisions*. Oxford: Basil Blackwell.

Kakabadse, A. (1984) *The Politics of Management*. Aldershot: Gower.

Kakabadse, A. (1991) *The Wealth Creators*. London: Kogan Page.

Levicki, C. J. (1996) *The Strategy Workout*. London: FT Pitman Publishing.

Moore, C. L. (1984) *Executives in Action*. Plymouth: Macdonald & Evans Ltd.

Peter, L. J. and Hull, R. (1979) *The Peter Principle*. London: Pan.

Pettigrew, A. M. (1973) *The Politics of Organizational Decision-Making*. London: Tavistock.

Biographies of companies and leaders

Burrough, D. and Jelyar, J. (1990) *Barbarians at the Gate*. London: Jonathan Cape.

Eberts, J. and Ilott, T. (1990) *My Indecision is Final*. London: Faber & Faber.

Gittin N. and Masters, K. (1997) *Hit and Run*. New York: Simon & Schuster.

Love, J. F. (1995) *McDonald's: Behind the Arches*. New York: Bantam.

Malik, R. (1975) *And Tomorrow the World?* London: Millington.

Sloan, A. P. (1965) *My Years with General Motors*. New York: MacFadden-Bartell.

Thompson, P. (1990) *Sharing the Success*. London: Fontana.

THE
CHROMOSOMES
OF LEADERSHIP

....

This chapter defines the key rules for a great

leadership career. It describes how they work

and how to ensure you apply them to your

career. And, finally, it reveals the

'leadership gene'.

....

A MODERN VIEW OF CHROMOSOMES

One dictionary definition of 'chromosome' is: 'any of several threadlike bodies, consisting of chromatin, that are found in a cell nucleus and carry the genes in a linear order; so-called because the chromosomes take on colour when a cell is stained.'

If the gene of leadership is, as this book argues, housed within the leader at birth, the chromosomes form the threads of the leader's development,

> Are you prepared to do *everything* it will take to become a great leader, especially the imposition of great self discipline?

both as a child and throughout the early evolution of their psyche. It is these threads that give colour to the leadership gene. The gene is only the starting point, the vital progenitor of many ingredients that have to be in place before the creation of a quality leader is completed.

Modern technology, particularly biotechnology, has developed the means to create life itself. Sheep can be cloned, DNA can be reproduced and the basic structures of life can be engendered. Does this still mean, as the title of this book suggests, that leaders have to be born and cannot be made? In this final chapter I set out a summary of the essential features of leadership. Some seem to require, a purely genetic gift; to the reader, others may seem to be acquirable. It's only the reader's view that counts … Are *you* a great leader, now or in the future? Do you have the genes? Are you prepared to do *everything* it will take to become a great leader, especially the imposition of great self discipline? How do you intend to acquire the features of leadership? What have the question-naires you have (I hope) completed throughout this book told you about your current and potential leadership potential? If you have read as far as this chapter, you must still believe you have what it takes.

Chromosome 1: *Youthful energy*

Great leaders need youthful energy, all their working lives. It is frequently remarked about successful leaders that they seem to have enough energy for all their team. They exude youthfulness. Is this because leadership jobs are unusually invigorating or because people with an abnormal energy level rise to the top? The latter would be genetic, the former a consequence of leadership, rather than a cause.

I stated earlier that people who become great leaders often seem to have been emotionally mature all their lives. In Chapter 3 I advised you to focus on becoming emotionally mature, as young as possible. Maturity was defined as being able to understand people and events better, earlier, and with deeper insight, than others, who only seem to grasp what makes people tick later in life. A key trick of maturing early is to develop and exploit helicoptering skills and a long time horizon.

An adjunct to chromosome 1 (youthful energy) is to believe in yourself and start your leadership career while young, if you can. Mature and become wise, especially emotionally, by exercising your abilities to rise above any situation you are in at work, and see everything with perspective. Try to see situations from the point of view of your immediate boss or his or her leader. Put every ounce of energy into everything you do, as if it's the last job you'll ever have and the last day you'll spend on earth. Release your genetic energy. You'll find it gets replaced with more, and then more again. Energy may be a genetic gift. It helps if you are born with it. But if you aren't, make it your personal habit.

Being emotionally mature is sometimes seen as 'having an old head on young shoulders'. But, at the end of the late 20th century, 'being young' has become highly desirable as a quality in its own right. When I visit clients in the USA I often wonder, 'whatever happened to grey hair?'. Even octogenarians seem to have a full head of lustrous, grey-free, hair. I have wondered whether it is just me who has become prematurely grey. However, I then remembered that President Reagan had legitimized the use of hair colouring for men. Men don't accept grey any more! There are also more valid reasons for people wanting to look young. The young have qualities that are highly desirable. They have energy, optimism, and a passion for life, because they have all their virginal expectations before them. That is both a worthwhile and a desirable state. If you can aim for it, and try to stay like that throughout your life, then go for it. It is not only good for leaders, it's highly desirable for anybody. However, it is particularly useful for leaders to try to retain their youthfulness, because they need energy, and all the other qualities of youth, with which to inspire their followers. The young enjoy life. Leaders should enjoy their work. Energy and youth, as well as physical health, make the mind work better. Above all, the young have optimism; leaders need to be optimistic, too, to engender belief in the success of their policies.

If youthfulness can be aligned with the wisdom of greater emotional maturity, one has a perfect combination. Recent research (*see* Goleman 1996; Cooper and Sawaf 1997) shows that both emotional maturity and empathy can be more important than pure analytical intelligence, as tools of leadership.

> You have to believe in yourself, without arrogance. Try to prepare yourself and be ready for the next job you aspire to, while striving for total competence in whatever you are doing now. Whatever job you gain, do it with distinction.

You have to believe in yourself, without arrogance. Try to prepare yourself and be ready for the next job you aspire to, while striving for total competence in whatever you are doing now. Whatever job you gain, do it with distinction. It matters not if it's waiting on tables during your university vacation, or working on the shop floor during an apprenticeship. Bring the same impeccable standards to all situations.

It's always appropriate to wear clothes that fit the role, so dress the part and don't be shy about doing so. Never *over*dress for the part – wearing an MD's shirt when you are the area manager may annoy some MDs. Always do the right deed (guided by your conscience) and never countenance contempt for the managers you are passing as you move up the organization. Your excellent brain and aptitude for leadership are just accidents of birth, with no more merit than if you had been born tall or handsome. Be grateful for your good luck.

Chromosome 2: *Courageous circumspection*

No matter how many leadership qualities and skills you have, your career will still be subject to accidents, luck and circumstances. You will need a sense of circumspection to help you cope with the worst which is coming your way. What will the worst look like?

- idiots getting jobs you could do ten times better
- malicious conduct by lesser mortals

- jealousy from those who wish they were as bright as you
- sabotage from corporate vandals
- the existence of so many more fools than bright people.

You'll need lots of courage too, because most good things won't come easily. There will be setbacks, crises, bad luck. You will have to face terrible dilemmas where there is no one to give you answers and everything is your own responsibility. Imagine, for example, the day when you are facing a major takeover bid with thousands of *your* people's jobs at stake, with all of them dependent on you getting it right. How will you handle the crisis? What priorities will receive your attention first? What will you do to ensure that every aspect of your beliefs and your duties receive the right consideration, your best judgement and the most apt answers? Whatever conclusion you draw and whichever way you go, some people out there won't think you are the great leader you are reputed to be. And you won't feel that you are either.

> Whatever conclusion you draw and whichever way you go, some people out there won't think you are the great leader you are reputed to be.

That is why you will need courageous circumspection. If you diligently and consistently put in the right inputs, and take ethically and strategically sound decisions at every step of the path, you will arrive at optimal solutions. But if it doesn't come out right, circumspection will help you to cope, because, being wise, you will judge yourself by your own standards. You will know that the pleasure is, truly, in the journey as much as the arrival. And if you enjoy *all* the journey, but don't quite make it to the final job you aspire to, circumspection will ensure that you will have had almost all the fun anyway. It will be just the accolade of the final job you will have missed. It won't feel so bad or so important.

Courage is vital in a leader because there will always be tough tasks to carry out. Among the toughest will be telling people you are taking their employment away from them, for the greater good of the organization. Some day your duty may lead you to close factories and ruin whole towns. At another time, your board of directors will treat you badly and may ask you to step down, or a competitor may buy the company you work for and decide they do not need you! You must hope that you did it better to others than they will do it to you. Your courage will be fully tested. You will need courage because there is no point to being frightened; no one can never predict the weird events that will happen to you during your career. Neither can you forsee the wonderful things that may evolve. Fear should not be part of your psychological make-up. It has little purpose. A little rational apprehension might usefully keep you on your guard. But don't be fearful – it's a waste of energy.

Remember the helicopter tool. It will help you keep events in perspective. Whenever you face important or dramatic moments, whether in your personal or your business life, jump into the helicopter and get your perspective back. If you find the helicopter is out of action, turn to the time-horizon machine. Ask yourself how awful will this situation feel in three months, three years, 30 years time? There will always be some length of time horizon where the pain will not cause so much anguish.

Beware when your temper takes over. It will curtail circumspection and cripple your courage. Be cautious when large events loom in your business career. Be careful at times when you feel fear – it distorts your vision and belittles your character. Fear is always a consequence of not thinking a problem through clearly. When you do, everything will fall into perspective and you will then be able to summon the necessary brain power to deal with the problem. If it's a business problem, then assemble enough merchant bankers, consultants, colleagues, friends and trustees to deal with it. Every problem can be broken into enough constituent parts to get it solved. If its a personal problem you may need to use different methods. First, share it with a friend – that always helps. Second, sleep on it – the subconscious mind often finds solutions that willed concentration cannot determine. Third, if necessary, get objective help from professionals who specialize in your problem, whether it's emotional, physical or just life.

Chromosome 3: *Winning ways*

How can you know, in advance, that you have winning ways and can arrive at the very top of the organization? You must plan a total career on the assumption that you *will* win. You have to ignore the danger that you may end your career thwarted by circumstances and bad luck. Plan it and you will win; wing it and you will weaken. Most leaders with winning ways map out their life-plan, as fully as possible. Many who aspire to the top echelons, won't make it. By definition, there will always be some dis-appointed aspirants to leadership! If you're looking for sympathy, you won't find it in this book!

One of the keys to giving your winning ways chromosome the chance to weave its magic for you, is to plan your total career, as young as pos-sible. The most brilliant careers come out best if they are planned that way. After all, there is nothing lost if it doesn't come out the way you design, particularly if you hold your own counsel and don't tell anybody. A total plan will help you to keep events in perspective, when your career suffers the accidents that will form the best part of your maturation. All careers take longer to come to fruition than one wants. Don't be tempted to take short cuts, which are unworthy of you, to get to the top earlier than is your due. If you always place your career in a total context, you'll remember to go slowly when you must. Get the important things right. You don't want to get to the top, at long last, and have journalists research your résumé and dig out some bankruptcy you presided over 20 years ago which you hoped was buried and forgotten.

Chromosome 4: *Balance*

During your successful career you will put a lot of thought into getting the right jobs, taking the correct strategic decisions and choosing the best members of your business team. Finding a suitable partner to share your life must be worth an equal amount of time and effort.

Throughout this book, I have argued from a base of personal philosophy and belief that a leader needs to have a bal-anced mixture of business interests and private life, humanity and ruthlessness, subjectivity and objectivity. Too much emphasis on one will lessen the success and fulfilment of the other. Nobody can tell any leader what their perfect bal-ance should be. But they will know when they are unbalanced. I argued in Chapter 3 that you can do something about it and described some of the necessary techniques. You will savour it when you are running a rounded life – your triumphs will feel fabulous. When they don't, it's because they are not in the context of a balanced life.

Try not to lose the good habits of your youth, such as finding time for sport, social life and recreation. Build opportunities for leisure into your timetable, in as disciplined a way as possible, as you construct your business diary. When there is fun available at work, enjoy it as a pleasure, rather than endure it as a chore. Find a partner to share your life, after you have enjoyed the first successes of your career. You may be too busy for the first five to ten years, many leaders are. But after that, get on with it. When you are ready to begin the search for that perfect partner, enjoy the best quality 'market research', and select wisely. During your successful career you will put a lot of thought into getting the right jobs, taking the correct strategic decisions and choosing the best members of your business team. Finding a suitable partner to share your life must be worth an equal amount of time and effort.

Chromosome 5: *Intuition*

Case study 8.1

HEARING AND SEEING INTUITIVELY

A little while ago we had a sad event in my family. My father-in-law died. I flew out to the USA to attend the funeral and to be with my wife who had been with him when he died. Our little son, was, we considered, too young to attend a funeral; he was only five years old. So we asked some friends in the UK to look after him, while we were away in the USA. On the day of the funeral in the USA, our son was out walking with our friends in Oxford in the UK. Our friend asked Jeffrey why he was looking so sad (we had asked that he should not be told of the death of his grandfather until we arrived home to tell him ourselves). Our little son replied to our friend, 'I can hear crying in America'. Perhaps he was in touch with his intuition ...

That story about my son illustrates the kind of intuition that all who aspire to be great must engage. At the end of the day, if you retain the magic and mystery of your intuition, you will value it for the insights it gives you. It is the ultimate dimension, a genetic tool. Whoever, or whatever, invented human beings, gave them an astonishing capacity to sense the right way forward. Intuition goes beyond rational thought. It is intimately connected to the sources of survival. Becoming sophisticated and civilized can sometimes get between you and your innate intuition and instincts. But, if, like my five-year-old son, you can stay in touch with your intuition, you will enhance your chances of success!

Chromosome 6: *Moral fibre*

Up to this point, the summation of the power of the chromosomes of leadership could have described an accomplished monster or a luminary leader. The essential difference between a great leader and a dangerous master is the vital ingredient of moral fibre. I discussed above the philosophical underpinning of the vital requirement of morality in a leader's personal and business life. Now I am going further. I believe that without moral fibre, a leader is both worthless and dangerous. It doesn't matter that they can make more money for the shareholders, if they make it immorally. It is irrelevant if they can build great empires for Mammon, if their morality is missing. Moral fibre protects the individual from the devil within himself and the organization from the effects of a vacuous lack of moral guidelines. If you don't find your genetic moral fibre on your first inspection, keep searching – its discovery may be your salvation.

> The essential difference between a great leader and a dangerous master is the vital ingredient of moral fibre.

Chromosome 7: *Leadership*

This book has brought together all the ingredients necessary to make a fine leader. I have described the skills, the traits, the characteristics and the styles of leaders. I have listed the tools and the time horizons, the measures and the means. When you ponder on the chromosomes described above, you may consider that you need to be born with some of them. You may decide that others are accrued during childhood, through development and environment. It is my final assertion that by the time leaders start their career, they will need to have assembled, if they are going to make it to the top, all the 'chromosomes' of leadership. There will still be some who fail, because bad luck will louse up their best opportunity. Others will stumble because they fail to match up to the awesome challenge of leadership, either through individual incapacity or factors of fate. But for those who are going to make it to the very top of an organization, by the time they begin their career, if they are to succeed they will need to have assembled a full complement of the chromosomes of *the leadership gene*.

RECOMMENDED READING FOR CHAPTER 8

Campbell, A., M., Devine, M. and Young, D. (1990) *A Sense of Mission* London: Hutchinson.

Cooper, R. and Sawaf, A. (1997) *Executive EQ*. London: Orion Business Books.

Covey, S. R. (1989) *The 7 Habits of Highly Effective People*. New York: Simon & Schuster.

Ferrucci, P. (1990) *What We May Be*. London: Aquarian/Thorsons.

Goleman, D. (1996) *Emotional Intelligence*. London: Bloomsbury.

Hamel, G. and Prahalad, C. K. (1994) *Competing for the Future*. Cambridge, MA: Harvard Business School.

Herder, J. (1992) *The Tao of Leadership*. Aldershot: Gower.

Koch, R. and Campbell, A. (1994) *Wake Up and Shake Your Company*. London: Pitman Publishing.

Peter, L. J. and Hull, R. (1979) *The Peter Principle*. London: Pan.

Peters, T. J. and Waterman, R. H., Jr. (1982) *In Search of Excellence*. New York: Harper & Row.

White, R. P., Hodgson, P. and Crainer, S. (1996) *The Future of Leadership*. London: Pitman Publishing.

Biographies of companies and leaders

Bayer, T. (1991) *Maxwell: The Outsider*. London: Mandarin.

Bramson, A. (1990) *Pure Luck*. Wellingborough: Patrick Stephens.

Colier, P. and Horowitz, D. (1976) *The Rockefellers*. New York: Signet.

Davies, H. (1981) *The Grades*. London: Weidenfeld & Nicolson.

Heller, R. (1993) *The Super Chiefs*. New York: Truman Talley/Plume.

Kessler, R. (1987) *Khashoggi*. London: Corgi.

Lenzner, R. (1985) *The Great Getty*. New York: Signet.

McLachlan, S. (1983) *The National Freight Buy-Out*. London: MacMillan.

Morita, A. (1994) *Made in Japan*. London: HarperCollins.

Shawcross, W. (1992) *Murdoch*. London: Chatto & Windus.

Thompson, P. (1990) *Sharing the Success*. London: Fontana.

Vanderbilt, A., II (n.d.) *Fortune's Children*. Falmouth: Sphere.

Walton, S. (1993) *Made in America*. New York: Bantam.

Wanstell, G. (1987) *Tycoon*. London: Grafton.

INDEX

Page numbers in *italics* refer to tables and diagrams, those in **bold** to case studies.